HOOKED ON LANGUAGE ARTS!

Ready-to-Use Activities and Worksheets for Grades 4–8

Judie L. H. Strouf

**THE CENTER FOR APPLIED
RESEARCH IN EDUCATION**
West Nyack, New York 10995

10 9 8 7 6 5 4 3 2 1

Library of Congress Cataloging-in-Publication Data

Strouf, Judie L. H.
    Hooked on language arts! : Ready-to-use worksheets
    and activities
    For grades 4–8 / Judie L. H. Strouf.
        p.   cm.   0-87628-403-9
        ISBN
        1. Language arts (Elementary—Study and teaching—
    Handbooks,manuals, etc.   2. Teaching—Handbooks,
    manuals, etc.   3. Teaching—Aids and devices—Handbooks,
    manuals, etc.   4. Activity programs in education—
    Handbooks, manuals, etc.   I. Title
    LB1576.S855 1990
    372.6′044—dc20   90–47637
                                                            CIP

**THE CENTER FOR APPLIED
RESEARCH IN EDUCATION**
BUSINESS & PROFESSIONAL DIVISION
A division of Simon & Schuster
West Nyack, New York 10995

Printed in the United States of America

DEDICATION

To busy teachers everywhere
to lighten their loads
and brighten their days.

ACKNOWLEDGMENTS
Clip art from Dover Clip Art Series
and Dover Pictorial Archive Series,
by permission of
Dover Publications, Inc., Mineola, New York

About the Author

JUDIE L. H. STROUF attained her teaching certificate and B. S. in English from Central Michigan University, Mount Pleasant, Michigan. She also earned an M. A. in K-12 Guidance and Counseling from Western Michigan University in Kalamazoo. She taught and/or counseled for twenty-seven years, the last twenty at Harbor Springs Schools in Michigan.

Judie has a varied background, having taught middle school /junior high language arts, reading, English, drama, speech, and social studies, as well as high school English, remedial reading, journalism, literature, advanced composition, creative writing, grammar, and special education. She served in several junior and senior high schools as counselor, Dean of Girls, and Guidance Director, and supervised numerous student teachers.

Recipient of the Fulbright Scholarship Award, she spent one year as an exchange teacher and acting English Department Head at Chipping Norton Grammar School in England. Here she taught both "school leavers" and university-bound Britons, and supervised student teachers from Oxford University. She has traveled extensively on three continents, most recently vacationing in Kenya.

Judie is part of a teaching family. Her parents, husband of thirty-eight years, and both children are teachers. She currently resides in Harbor Springs.

About This Resource

Getting students hooked on language arts is like preparing nutritious meals. You need fresh and appealing appetizers to stimulate interest, solid main courses to satisfy hunger, and pleasing desserts for fun. You want to make language arts go down easily, but be nourishing as well.

Even with extensive planning, skill, and patience, you don't always come up with delicious fare. You can, however, get most students "hooked" if you carefully provide them with what they need and want: motivational introductions to lessons; imaginative assignments; and amusing, yet educational, diversions for fun. You can supply action, humor, and variety to make learning simpler and more stimulating. Using the ideas here, you can, indeed, satisfy your students' intellectual appetites.

This book is an ideal collection of EASY-TO-USE and TIME-SAVING educational games, gimmicks, and "gotchas" for grades 4–8. The activities take *minimal* teacher preparation, energy, and imagination, yet provide that extra punch to captivate and educate. You can use them "as is," or adapt them to accommodate your unique class and teaching style.

We emphasize four major language arts areas:

- Writing and Composition
- Reading and Literature
- Words and Sentences
- Speaking, Listening, and Oral Presentation

Simply turn to the appropriate section in the book before planning your lessons in that area and discover a motivational jackpot! (The relegation of topics to a particular section is arbitrary. In practice, there is a close interrelationship among all language arts areas, and most techniques can and *should* be integrated.)

Preceding each idea is a key word (INTRO, FOCUS, or JOKER) for quick visual guidance. You can save valuable time by observing the markers to help you find the exact type of activity you need.

INTRO stands for introductory ideas. These include openers, lesson-beginners, interest-piquers, attention-getters, and curiosity-arousers for use when introducing a topic. The INTRO activity serves as the appetizer for the lesson, and is most often used at the beginning of a lesson.

FOCUS indicates high-interest, student-involving, intriguing assignments. These are lessons concerning a main topic or concept in language arts. Here you will find the "meat" of the main course—something for students to mentally chew on and digest.

JOKER precedes items added for variety and pleasure. Thus, JOKER marks games, riddles, puzzles, and fun activities for drill, practice, and review. This is the dessert!

An extensive TABLE OF CONTENTS lists main topics or concepts with specific names of activities and ideas under each. (Many activities cover additional concepts, but this will help you "zero in" on what you need.) All 129 reproducible worksheets contain an asterisk (*) at the beginning and end of their titles for easy identification throughout the book. In addition, the FAST REPRODUC-IBLE FINDER in the frontmatter indexes all reproducible worksheets and activities alphabetically by page number.

This book is predicated upon the belief that motivation is the key to learning. The finest motivation, of course, is intrinsic; it comes from within the students. In most classrooms, however, *you* have to nurture, kindle, and ignite that drive which often lies dormant in upper elementary, middle, and junior high youngsters. This compendium will help you provide these opportunities EASILY and QUICKLY.

It is often difficult to discern where ideas originate. Through years of teaching, reading, discussions with other teachers, workshops, seminars, and observations of student teachers, you borrow, adapt, and develop a repertoire of approaches that work. If, by chance, techniques in this collection rightfully "belong" to someone else, it is inadvertent. May you use them so frequently with success that they also become an integral part of YOU!

Judie L. H. Strouf

Table of Contents

About the Author (iv)

About This Resource (v)

Fast Reproducible Finder (xvi)

SECTION I: WRITING AND COMPOSITION (1)

Autobiography

ME (3)

Choppiness

CHOP CHOP (3) *BABY WRITING* (4) CORRECTING CHOPPY STYLE (5)

Clarity

BE, CLEAR DEAR (5) *BE, CLEAR DEAR* (6)

Comparison/ Contrast

MY SHADOW AND I (7) OPPOSITES ATTRACT (7) GETTING TO KNOW YOU (7) *GETTING TO KNOW YOU* (8) *SIMILARITIES/ DIFFERENCES PARAGRAPHS* (9)

Description

HOW LONG SHOULD IT BE? (10) LOOK/SEE (10) EXPERIENCE RE-CALL (10) WORD PICTURES (10) PICTURE PERFECT (11) MY FRIEND IS MISSING! (11)

Dialogue

MAG PICS (11) *MAG PICS DIALOGUE* (12) *MAG PIGS DIALOGUE HELPER SHEET* (13) FUNNY PAPERS (14)

Explanation

WHICH CAME FIRST—THE CHICKEN OR THE EGG? (15) *HOW DO I GET FROM HERE TO THERE?* (16) *THIS IS HOW YOU BAKE A CAKE * (17) *PROVERBIAL TRUTHS* (18)

* Reproducible activities.

Fable

TRICKY DICKY (19)   FABULOUS FABLES (21)

Image-builder

I'M REALLY A PRETTY GREAT PERSON (20)   WRITING CONTESTS (21)   MOMENTOUS MILESTONES (21)

Imagination Development

HAPPY HOLIDAYS (21)   *HAPPY HOLIDAYS PLAN SHEET * (22)   ONCE UPON A TIME (23)   AND THEN . . . (24)   THREE THINGS THEREIN (25)   *MAKE A CONNECTION* (26)

Interview

I DIDN'T KNOW THAT! (27)   *I DIDN'T KNOW THAT!* (28)

Journal

DAILY JOURNALS (29)   COOPERATIVE JOURNAL ENTRIES (30)

Letter

ENVELOPE ENIGMA (30)   *LETTER LITERACY* (31)   V.I.P. VISITOR (32)

Mood Creation

MAGNIFICENT MAGNIFICATION (32)   PUT ME IN THE MOOD (32)   *PUT ME IN THE MOOD* (33)

Newspaper

NEWSPAPER KNOWLEDGE (34)   NEWS HOUND (34)   *NEWSPAPER KNOWLEDGE* (35)   CLASSY NEWSPAPER (36)   OBSERVER TREPI-DATION (36)   *CLASSY NEWSPAPER* (37)

Note-taking

MONKEY DO; MONKEY WRITE (38)

Opinion Defense

DEVIL'S ADVOCATE (38)   *DEFEND YOURSELF* (39)

Outlining

SCRAMBLED EGGS (41)

Penmanship

ILLEGIBILITY (42)   PENMANSSSSSHIP (42)   *PENMANSSSSSHIP * (43)

Personal Experience

LIKE-DISLIKE (45)   *DOT DOT DOT* (46)

Poetry

LIMERICKING AROUND THE ROOM (47)   NAME RIDDLE (47)

NAME THAT POEM (47)   *NAME THAT POEM * (48)   LYRIC POEM (49)
LYRIC POEM READING (51)   MUSICAL MOTIF (41)

Proofreading and Rewriting

MUFFED UP—WHAT NOW? (51)   *PROOF IS IN THE PUDDING* (52)
WRITING TO RHYTHM (53)

Report

RANDOM REPORTS (54)

Research

OCCUPATIONS OCTOPUS (54)   *OCCUPATIONS OCTOPUS* (55)

Senses Development

TUNING UP YOUR SENSES (56)

Sequence

MIXED-UP (56)

Solution to Problem or Dilemma

SET-UP (57)   *EYE WITNESS* (58)   *WHAT SHOULD YOU DO?*(59)

Story

MONSTER MADNESS (60)   ABSTRACT ATTRACTIONS (61)   INK
BLOTS (61)   SNIP-SNIP (61)   DRIBBLE PIC (61)   RUNAWAY PAINT
(62)   LAST STRAW (62)   ALL THUMBS (62)   *STRING-A-LING STORY*
(63)   CLAY CHARACTER (64)   CLASS BOOK (64)   ANIMALISMS (64)
ANIMALISMS (65)

Tall Tales and Topic Sentences

TELL A TALL ONE (66)   SHORT AND SWEET (66)   *A CAT'S TALE*
(67)   SHORT AND SWEET PARAGRAPHS (68)   VERY TOPICAL (68)

Wordiness

STRETCH LIMOUSINE (68)   *STRETCH LIMOUSINE* (70)

SECTION II: READING AND LITERATURE (71)

Advertisement

ANALYZING ADS (73)   ADVANCE PUBLICITY (73)   GOOD MORNING
(74)   *TANTALIZING ADS* (75)

Alliteration

DO YOU SEE WHAT I SEE? (76)   TONGUE-TWISTERS (76)   *ALLITER-
ATIVE ANECDOTE* (77)

Biography/ Autobiography

BIO/AUTOBIO (78)

Book Display

BOOK FAIR (78)

Book/ Story Report

NOVEL AND STORY REPORTS (78)   *NOVEL REPORT* (79)   *STORY REPORT* (80)   *WHAT I THINK ABOUT MY STORY* (81)   ALTERNATIVE BOOK REPORTS (82)   *DESCRIPTIONS* (83)   *AUTHOR REPORT* (84)   *CROSSWORD* (85)   *QUOTES* (86)   *ESSAY* (87)   *COMPARE/CONTRAST* (88)   *NEW VOCABULARY* (89)

Characterization

GUILTY OR INNOCENT (90)   *MAKE THE SCENE* (91)   WHO AM I? (92)

Comprehension

LISTEN FOR CLUES (92)   *SAME OR DIFFERENT?* (94)   *WHAT IS OUT OF PLACE* (94)

Fairy Tale

FAIRY TALE MAP   (95)

Fiction/ Non-Fiction

FICTION VERSUS NONFICTION (96)   FACT AND FICTION (96)

Following Directions

CAN YOU FOLLOW DIRECTIONS? (96)   *FOLLOWING DIRECTIONS (Easy paper/pencil version)* (97)   *FOLLOWING DIRECTIONS (Difficult paper/pencil version)* (98)   *FOLLOWING DIRECTIONS (Physical directions version)* (100)

Foreshadowing

CASTING SHADOWS (101)

Guest

SURPRISE GUEST (101)

Hyperbole

EXAGGERATION (102)

Image-builder

GOOD DEEDS BOX (102)   BOOKWORM (102)

Imagery

SENSE APPEAL (103)

Inference

JACK AND JILL (104)   WILL THE YOUNGEST PLEASE STAND UP? (104)   *YOUNG AND OLD, OR IN-BETWEEN?* (105)

Library

LIBRARY TRIP (106)   FIVE-FINGER RULE (106)   CARD CATS (106)   *CARD CATS* (107)   *LIBRARY LOCATION SKILLS* (108)

Literary Terminology (General)

SIZZLE (109)   *SIZZLE PREP SHEET* (110)   *SIZZLE EXAMPLES* (112)

Magazine

ROOM MAG COLLECTION (113)   MAGAZINE SUMMARY (113)   *MAG-
AZINE SUMMARY* (114)

Main Idea and Note-taking

HEADLINES (115)   NOTE-TAKING (115)   WEBBING (115)   *CATS*
(116)   *NOTE-TAKING (OUTLINE SYSTEM)* (117)   *NOTE-TAKING
(BOX SYSTEM)* (118)

Poetry

POETRY MAP (119)   POETRY READING (120)   RHYME TIME (120)
INCOMPLETE RHYMES (120)   *ADD-A-LETTER RHYME* (121)

Research

RESEARCH FLOW CHART (122)   *RESEARCH REPORT WEB* (123)
REPORTING ON RESEARCH (124)

Serial Story

ONE DAY AT A TIME (124)

Simile/Metaphor

SAY WHAT? (125)

Skimming and Speed Reading

SKIM THE NEWS (126)   SPEED READ (126)   *SPEEDY READERS*
(127)

Time Line

STUDENT TIME LINE (128)

SECTION III   WORDS AND SENTENCES (129)

Abbreviation

LIST OF COMMON ABBREVIATIONS (131)   *ABOMINABLE ABBRE-
VIATIONS * (134)   *ABBREVIATION VARIATION* (135)   *STATE IT*
(136)

Affix

FAST AFFIXES (137)   GUESS THE PREFIX OR SUFFIX (137)   *GUESS
THE AFFIX* (138)   *COMMON ROOTS AND AFFIXES* (139)

Alphabetizing

CLASS ALPHABET (140)   ROOM ALPHABET (140)

Anagram

ANAGRAM ANOMALY (141)   *CAN A CAT BECOME A DOG? (142)

Antonym

*GETTING ACQUAINTED WITH ANTONYMS (143)

Capitalization

GETTING BRANDED (144)

Connotation/ Denotation

*CONNOTATION CONNECTIONS (146)

Cryptogram

CAN YOU DE-CODE DE CODE? (147)   *MIND-BOGGLERS* (148)

Diacritical Mark

USING THE MACRON AND BREVE (149)   *USING THE SCHWA* (150)

Dictionary

DICTIONARY JOKE (151)   DICTIONARY RACE (151)

Etymology

ETYMOLOGIES (152)   *INTERESTING ETYMOLOGIES* (153) *WHERE DID THE WORDS COME FROM?* (154)

Grammar

BASIC SENTENCE PATTERNS (156)   SUBJECT/VERB RIDDLE (157)   WHAT'S THE OBJECT? (157)   HOW DO YOU FEEL ABOUT HARRY? (157)   BLANK THE BUILDING (158)   INTERJECT YOUR EMOTION (159)   *PRE-POSITION THE PREPOSITION* (160)   DING-A-LING (161)   SUPER ACTION MAN (161)   ADVERB INTRODUCTION (161)   *ACTION MAN CAN* (162)   MISSING PARTS (163)   NOUN BALL (163)   GRAMMAR UP (164)   CONJUNCTION JUNCTION (164)   *PRO-CROSS* (166)   *PLAIN JANE* (167)

Homonym

SOUND ALIKES (168)

Idiosyncracy (Word and Letter)

DOUBLE TROUBLE (169)   *ALPHABET SOUP* (170)   *WORDS WITHIN WORDS* (171)   *RIDDLE FUN* (172)

Palindrome

PALINDROME PALS (173)

Plural

PLURAL PICS (173)

Pronunciation

PRONUNCIATION FUN (173)

Punctuation

PUNCTUATION RIDDLE (174)   CLASSIC PUNCTUATION PUZZLE (174)   I NEED A COMMA! (175)   PHONETIC PUNCTUATION (175)   EX-AGGERATED PUNCTUATION (175)

Spelling

HARD SPELL (176)   SPELLING PRACTICE (177)   SPELL REVIEW (177)   KINESTHETIC SPELLING (177)   WORDLE (178)   SPELLDOWN WITH A TWIST (178)

Syllable

SYLLABLE RIDDLES (178)   BEAT THE RHYTHM (179)   CLASSROOM SYLLABLES (179)

Synonym/ Vocabulary

FLASH CARD VOCAB (180)   VOCAB BINGO (180)   *VOCAB BINGO* (182)

SECTION IV: SPEAKING, LISTENING, AND ORAL PRESENTATION (183)

Choral Reading

CHORAL READING (185)   *THE RAVEN* (186)   *THE RAVEN VOCAB HELPER *(190)   *RAPPING* (192)

Communication

COMMUNICATION SCRAMBLE (193)

Cooperative Interaction

DON'T REPEAT THIS, BUT . . . (194)   PARTNER PANTOMINE (194) THERE'LL BE SOME CHANGES MADE (195)   ALL TALK (195)   ORAL STORY GAMES (195)

Debate/ Discussion

CLASS DISCUSSION (196)   MINI-DEBATES (197)   *MINI-DEBATING* (198)

Diorama

MAKE A DIORAMA (197)

Image-builder

MIKE MAGIC (197)   BULLETIN BOARD IDEA (199)   THANK-YOU BOX (199)   STORY TIME (199)   *STORY TIME* (200)

Pantomine/ Skit

STAGE FRIGHT ELIMINATOR (201)   *CHARADES* (202)   FOLLOW THE LEADER (203)   MIRROR MIME (203)   OBJECT PANTOMIME (204)   FABLE PANTOMIME (204)   FIRST PANTOMIME (204)   *EASY PANTOMIME TOPICS* (205)   *LET'S PRETEND* (206)   PUPPETS ON

A STICK (207)   DISGUISE YOURSELF (207)   PUTTIN' ON THE SKITS
(208)   *TAG-LINERS* (209)   *QUOTABLE QUOTES* (210)   *HANDY-
DANDY* (211)   *TRICKY IMPROV* (212)

Sound Effect

EFFECTIVE SOUNDS (213)   SILLY SOUNDS (213)   *SILLY SOUNDS
STORY* (214)

Speech

HOW-TO SPEECH (215)   *IMPROMPTU SPEECH* (216)   *ACCEPT-
ING AN AWARD* (217)   *ORAL REPORT* (218)   *ENCYCLOPEDIA
TALK* (219)   *NEWSPAPER REPORT* (220)   *RECITATION* (221)
TRUST ME—I'M RIGHT (222)

Stage

MAKE A THEATER (223)   COSTUMES (223)   *STAGE DIRECTIONS*
(224)

Teaching

TEACHER FOR A DAY (225)   *TEACHER FOR A DAY* (226)

Telephone Use

MA BELL (227)   *HELLO, AUTHOR* (228)

TV/ Radio/ Video

RADIO OR TV BROADCAST (229)   *TELEVISION ANALYSIS* (230)

Voice Expression

IT ISN'T WHAT YOU SAY—IT'S HOW (231)

SECTION V: ANSWER KEY (233)

Writing and Composition

BE, CLEAR DEAR (235)   *WHICH CAME FIRST—THE CHICKEN OR
THE EGG?* (235)   *LETTER LITERACY* (235)   *SCRAMBLED EGGS
(unscrambled)* (236)   *NAME THAT POEM* (236)   *PROOF IS IN THE
PUDDING* (236)

Reading and Literature

SAME OR DIFFERENT (236)   *WHAT IS OUT OF PLACE?* (236)
FOLLOWING DIRECTIONS (Easy paper/pencil version) (237)   *FOLLOW-
ING DIRECTIONS (Difficult paper/pencil version)* (237)   *YOUNG, OLD
OR IN-BETWEEN?* (237)   *CATS* (238) *INCOMPLETE RHYMES*
(239)   *ADD-A-LETTER RHYME* (239)

Words and Sentences

ABOMINABLE ABBREVIATIONS (239)   *ABBREVIATION VARIA-
TION* (239)   *STATE IT* (240)   *GUESS THE AFFIX* (240)   *COM-
MON ROOTS AND AFFIXES* (240)   *ANAGRAM ANOMALY* (241)
CAN A CAT BECOME A DOG? (241)   *GETTING AQUAINTED WITH

ANTONYMS* (241) *GETTING BRANDED* (241) *CAN YOU DE-
CODE DE CODE?* (242) *MIND-BOGGLERS* (242) *USING THE
SCHWA* (242) *BASIC SENTENCE PATTERNS* (242) *ACTION MAN
CAN* (242) *PRO-CROSS* (243) *DOUBLE TROUBLE* (243) *ALPHA-
BET SOUP* (243) *WORDS WITHIN WORDS* (243) *RIDDLE FUN*
(243)

Speaking, Listening, and Oral Presentation

COMMUNICATION SCRAMBLE (243)

Fast Reproducible Finder

Name of Worksheet	Page	Name of Worksheet	Page
A CAT'S TALE	67	ENCYCLOPEDIA TALK	219
ABBREVIATION VARIATION	135	ESSAY	187
ABOMINABLE ABBREVIATIONS	134	EYE WITNESS	58
		FAIRY TALE MAP	95
ACCEPTING AN AWARD	217	FOLLOWING DIRECTIONS (Difficult)	98
ACTION MAN CAN	162		
ADD-A-LETTER RHYME	121	FOLLOWING DIRECTIONS (Easy)	97
ALLITERATIVE ANECDOTE	77		
ALPHABET SOUP	170	FOLLOWING DIRECTIONS (Physical)	100
ALTERNATIVE BOOK REPORTS	82		
ANAGRAM ANOMALY	141	GETTING AQUAINTED WITH ANTONYMS	143
AND THEN . . .	24		
ANIMALISMS	65	GETTING BRANDED	144
AUTHOR REPORT	84	GETTING TO KNOW YOU	8
BABY WRITING	4	GUESS THE AFFIX	138
BASIC SENTENCE PATTERNS	156	GUILTY OR INNOCENT?	90
BE, CLEAR DEAR	6	HANDY DANDY	211
CAN A CAT BECOME A DOG?	142	HAPPY HOLIDAYS PLAN SHEET	22
CAN YOU DE-CODE DE CODE?	147	HELLO, AUTHOR	228
CARD CATS	107	HOW DO I GET FROM HERE TO THERE?	16
CATS	116		
CHARADES	202	HOW-TO SPEECH	215
CLASSY NEWSPAPER	37	I DIDN'T KNOW THAT!	28
COMMON ROOTS AND AFFIXES	139	IMPROMPTU SPEECH	216
COMMUNICATION SCRAMBLE	193	I'M REALLY A PRETTY GREAT PERSON	20
COMPARE/CONTRAST	88		
CONNOTATION CONNECTIONS	146	INTERESTING ETYMOLOGIES	153
CROSSWORD	85	IT ISN'T WHAT YOU SAY— IT'S HOW	231
DEFEND YOURSELF	39		
DESCRIPTIONS	83	LET'S PRETEND	206
DOT-DOT-DOT	46	LETTER LITERACY	31
DOUBLE TROUBLE	169	LIBRARY LOCATION SKILLS	108
EASY PANTOMIME TOPICS	205	LIKE-DISLIKE	45

Name of Worksheet	Page	Name of Worksheet	Page
LIST OF COMMON ABBREVIA-TIONS	131	SAY WHAT?	125
LYRIC POEM READING	50	SCRAMBLED EGGS	41
MA BELL	227	SILLY SOUNDS STORY	214
MAG PICS DIALOGUE	12	SIMILARITIES/DIFFERENCES PARAGRAPHS	9
MAG PICS DIALOGUE HELPER SHEET	13	SIZZLE EXAMPLES	112
MAGAZINE SUMMARY	114	SIZZLE PREP SHEET	110
MAKE A CONNECTION	26	SOUND-ALIKES	168
MAKE THE SCENE	91	SPEEDY READERS	127
MIND-BOGGLERS	149	STAGE DIRECTIONS	224
MINI-DEBATING	198	STATE IT	136
MONSTER MADNESS	60	STORY TIME	200
NAME THAT POEM	48	STORY REPORT	80
NEW VOCABULARY	89	STRETCH LIMOUSINE	70
NEWSPAPER KNOWLEDGE	35	STRING-A-LING STORY	63
NEWSPAPER REPORT	220	TAG-LINERS	209
NOTE-TAKING (BOX SYSTEM)	118	TANTALIZING ADS	75
NOTE-TAKING (OUTLINE SYSTEM)	117	TEACHER FOR A DAY	226
NOVEL REPORT	79	TELEVISION ANALYSIS	230
OCCUPATIONS OCTOPUS	55	THE RAVEN	186
ORAL REPORT	218	THE RAVEN VOCAB HELPER	190
PENMANSSSSSHIP	43	THIS IS HOW YOU BAKE A CAKE	17
PLAIN JANE	167	TRICKY IMPROV	212
POETRY MAP	119	TRUST ME—I'M RIGHT	222
PRE-POSITION THE PREPOSITION	160	USING THE MACRON AND BREVE	149
PRO-CROSS	160	USING THE SCHWA	150
PROOF IS IN THE PUDDING	52	VOCAB BINGO	182
PROVERBIAL TRUTHS	18	WHAT IS OUT OF PLACE	94
PUT ME IN THE MOOD	33	WHAT I THINK ABOUT MY STORY	81
QUOTABLE QUOTES	210	WHAT SHOULD YOU DO?	59
QUOTES	86	WHERE DID THE WORDS COME FROM?	154
RADIO OR TV BROADCAST	229	WHICH CAME FIRST—THE CHICKEN OR THE EGG?	15
RAPPING	192	WORDS WITHIN WORDS	171
RECITATION	221	WRITING TO RHYTHM	53
RESEARCH REPORT WEB	123	YOUNG, OLD, OR IN-BETWEEN?	105
RESEARCH FLOW CHART	122		
RIDDLE FUN	172		
SAME OR DIFFERENT	93		

Section I

WRITING AND COMPOSITION

JOKER   ME

Purpose: To use as a culminating activity after writing an autobiography to add importance, pride, and a degree of durability to the writing.

Use masking tape to attach scrap paper to the wall or chalkboard. Have the student sit in front of the paper with a lamp focussed so his silhouette shows against the paper. Trace the silhouette, and use it as a pattern. Trace the pattern onto construction paper, cut out, and carefully paste the cutout onto another sheet of contrasting colored paper. The traditional colors are black on white, but other combinations are effective, depending upon student preference and materials available. Students can assist each other in making the patterns.

Students delight in having these unique depictions of themselves as covers for their autobiographies. After adding another piece of construction paper for the back, they can use staples or paper fasteners (depending on type of paper used) to enclose their writing inside.

INTRO   CHOP-CHOP

Purpose: To introduce the monotony of short, choppy, unvaried sentences.

Say: Take out a piece of paper.
        Put your name on it.
        Number from one to five.
        Write these sentences.
        See Mary.
        See Tom.
        See Mary write.
        See Tom write.
        See Mary and Tom write.

Ask: Does anyone notice anything wrong with these sentences? (They will say they are "baby" sentences or "boring," etc.)

Agree with them, and point out this is called choppiness or immaturity in writing. After discussing how these sentences could be combined into a more interesting sentence, such as *Watch Mary and Tom while they write*, assign *BABY WRITING*.

Focus   *BABY WRITING*

Name _____   **Date** _____

   Purpose: To give practice in adding variety to sentences; to learn how to avoid choppy writing.

   Instructions: Write one paragraph in choppy sentences as a small child might. When finished, trade papers with the person next to you, and rewrite each other's baby writing so it is more grownup, less monotonous, and avoids choppiness. We will read both versions of several paragraphs aloud and discuss.

FOCUS   **CORRECTING CHOPPY STYLE**

Purpose: To give practice using connecting words to avoid a choppy writing style; to emphasize the importance of conjunctions.

Print the following conjunctions on small pieces of paper or poster board:

after	so that
although	since
if	whether
while	before
as	and
until	even though
when	but
because	or

Two copies of each word should handle an average-sized class. Use durable poster board if you want to use the words again for another group or for a different purpose later on.

Have each student draw one word (from a hat or from the face-down pile). On his paper he writes three sentences. The first two sentences are choppy and short, but related in content. The last sentence uses the "drawn" conjunction to correct the choppiness.

Students take turns reading their trio of sentences aloud. Discuss any incorrect sentences, eliciting ideas for improvement from the rest of the class.

Students seem to enjoy this method because the random drawing of words seems fun, they are not overwhelmed with a whole page of sentences at once, and they are interested in what their classmates wrote (instead of what they read from an impersonal book).

By the time each student finishes reading his sentences, the class has, however, had more practice and repetition than by completing the typical ten sentences in a text. In addition, you have the opportunity to see immediately if students are understanding the concept.

JOKER   **BE, CLEAR DEAR!**

Purpose: To stress clarity in writing; to have fun with unclear sentences.

Prepare ten sentences which are garbled or humorous because they lack clarity. The prepositional phrase may be in the wrong place, or a clause may modify the wrong sentence part. Ask students to change the sentences so they are clear. See *BE, CLEAR DEAR* for ready-made sentences.

Variation: Instruct *pairs* of students to make up two unclear sentences. Trade papers with a partner (another pair of students), each rewriting for more clarity.

Ask volunteers to read both versions to the class. These are often humorous and imaginative!

Joker   *BE, CLEAR DEAR*

Name _____   **Date** _____

Purpose: To stress clarity in writing; to have fun.

Instructions: On your own paper, change the following sentences into clearer ones that make sense.

1. At the age of ten my parents got divorced.

2. He bought a cat from a man that turned out to be a short-haired tabby.

3. I talked to a lady by the telephone pole that reminded me of you.

4. Since it was a sunny day, we ended up near the fountain sitting under an umbrella.

5. Long before Charlie had left everything to the brother he loved dearly.

6. The burly boy bumped into the elephant in a black hat.

7. The man's pig pen that used to be our friend was painted yesterday.

8. I walked along the dock as the boat sailed into port and swung my duffel bag.

9. The band played the school fight song just as the quiet lady opened the door with six trumpets.

10. The driver stopped his truck when the radiator boiled over and asked for water.

Water, please!

© 1990 by The Center for Applied Research in Education

FOCUS   MY SHADOW AND I

Purpose: To write a comparison showing the similarities between the student and another person in the room.

Instructions to students: Write three paragraphs about a person in this class who is most like you. Write three main ways you are alike, using details to support each way.

FOCUS   OPPOSITES ATTRACT

Purpose: To show a written contrast between the student and another person in the room.

Instructions to students: Write three paragraphs about a person in this class who is most unlike you. Write three main ways you are different, using details to support each way.

FOCUS   GETTING TO KNOW YOU

Purpose: To give practice in writing about similarities and differences; to construct a questionnaire; to write a well-organized paragraph using topic sentences; to increase self-image.

Elicit ideas from class for questions to ask: age, family size, placement in family (oldest, youngest, middle), hobbies, favorites (music, sports), unusual things that have happened to them, schools attended. Write them on the chalkboard as reminders.

Students make out questionnaires and give them to everyone in a certain row (or to students designated in an arbitrary way so that not just popular students are chosen). Students make up a separate sheet for each student interviewed with six questions and blank lines on which the interviewee writes his answers. All questions asked need not be the same, but three questions should be identical for every student in that particular row.

Every student makes up and answers questionnaires, the number depending upon the number of students in class, and how evenly you can divide them. In a class of 25 with rows of five students, each student makes up and answers four questionnaires. The lesson takes from two to four sessions depending upon student abilities. For student instructions, see *GETTING TO KNOW YOU* and *SIMILARITIES AND DIFFERENCES PARAGRAPHS*.

Variation: The composition requirements can be made more specific and difficult by designating a minimum length, requiring a rough draft, proofreading and rewrite, or assigning as homework.

Focus ***GETTING TO KNOW YOU***

Name _____ **Date** _____

Purpose: To construct a questionnaire to find out about similarities and differences of classmates; to answer a questionnaire; to increase self-image.

Instructions: Make up questionnaires to find similarities and differences among your classmates. You will be writing three paragraphs based on this information, using the worksheet, ***SIMILARITIES AND DIFFERENCES PARAGRAPHS***.

1. Use one sheet of paper for each student in your row, excluding yourself. (You need at least four other people, so if your row is short, add someone to total at least four.)

2. List six questions on each sheet with blank lines after each question for the respondent's answers. Use questions that will help you find out interesting and un-usual things about each student. Of the six questions, three should be identical for each person. The other questions should be different.

3. Write your name on the bottom of each sheet so the questionnaires will be returned to the right students.

4. Complete ALL your questionnaires before you give them to the people in your row.

5. Truthfully fill out all questionnaires given to you.

Purpose: To practice using the information gained from a questionnaire to write several well-organized paragraphs using appropriate topic sentences.

Instructions: Read the answers to the questions you asked the people in your row. You are looking for similarities and differences among the students who filled out your questionnaires. Then proceed to write three paragraphs as shown below.

1. Write a paragraph with the following topic sentence:

    The students in this row have many similar traits.

    IN THIS PARAGRAPH YOU WILL SHOW HOW THE STUDENTS ARE SIMILAR.

2. Write a paragraph with the following topic sentence:

    Although students seem to be very similar, individual traits do exist.

    IN THIS PARAGRAPH YOU WILL SHOW HOW INDIVIDUALS ARE DIFFERENT FROM EACH OTHER.

3. Write a paragraph with the following topic sentence:

    Students in the same row in our classroom share similar traits, but also differ in certain ways.

    IN THIS PARAGRAPH YOU WILL SUM UP THE LIKENESSES AND DIFFERENCES OF THE PEOPLE WHO ANSWERED YOUR QUESTIONNAIRES.

INTRO   **HOW LONG SHOULD IT BE?**

Purpose: To answer the *constant* student question about writing assignments ("How long should it be?").

Answer: Good writing should be like a skirt—long enough to cover the subject and short enough to be interesting!

FOCUS   **LOOK/SEE**

Purpose: To give written practice in accurate description.

Instructions to students: Look out the window, out the door, or around the room. Pick out one thing and write a description in a clear, concise paragraph. Do not name the object in the paragraph, but write it on the back of your paper.

After everyone is finished, have students read descriptions to the class. See if classmates can guess what is described.

FOCUS   **EXPERIENCE RECALL**

Purpose: To give written practice in recalling and describing accurately an experienced event.

Instructions to students: Write a paragraph describing an event you recently attended or in which you participated. Recall the details of the event, and write an accurate description. Examples: sports event, dance, party, meeting, concert, exhibit.

INTRO   **WORD PICTURES**

Purpose: To introduce descriptive writing.

Bring in four pictures of foreign or domestic scenes from outside the students' familiar geographic area. Before students enter the room, put pictures on chalk tray or in map clips. Label the pictures 1, 2, 3, and 4 for identification. Students will tend to browse around, discussing the pictures before being seated. Follow with PICTURE PERFECT.

Variation: Bring in pictures of people's faces or animals, slides, souvenirs, picture post cards, unusual clothes, photographs, or foods.

FOCUS　　　　　PICTURE PERFECT

Purpose: To provide practice in writing a description of a person, place, or thing. See WORD PICTURES.

Instructions to students: Write an accurate and complete description of one of the places shown in a picture. Guess what country or area of the United States the picture depicts. Put a number (1, 2, 3, or 4) on the back of your paper indicating which picture you are describing.

Variation: If using pictures of people's faces, ask students to write what the person is feeling; if using animal pictures, ask students to describe the animal. Students can write action stories instead of descriptions, using a place as a setting, or people and animals as characters. Alter instructions to suit the pictures.

FOCUS　　　　　MY FRIEND IS MISSING!

Purpose: To provide practice in writing a description of a real person.

Instructions to students: Imagine a friend has disappeared. The police contact you for an accurate description because no picture of the missing person is available. Describe your friend in such a detailed way that he or she will be located immediately. Put the name of the student you are describing on the back of your paper. We will guess who it is by the accuracy of your writing.

INTRO AND FOCUS　　　　MAG PICS

Purpose: To provide an incentive for writing dialogue; to provide the characters who will be speaking; to serve as an introduction to a lesson reviewing the use of quotation marks.

Collect a multitude of magazines. They need not be current. Distribute two magazines and a pair of scissors to each student. Let them browse until they find two or three pictures of people that appeal to them. Don't tell students how they will use the pictures.

Instructions to students: Find two or three pictures of people in the magazines, cut them out, and paste them on your paper. When everyone has finished, I'll tell you what we are going to use them for. Distribute copies of worksheets, *MAG PICS DIALOGUE* and *MAG PICS DIALOGUE HELPER SHEET*.

Variation: Use the magazine picture to illustrate your story, not necessarily the characters, but perhaps the setting, conflict, or one of the incidents.

Focus   ***MAG PICS DIALOGUE***

Name _____   **Date** _____

Purpose: To practice writing dialogue; to use magazine characters who will be speaking; to review quotation marks.

Instructions: Paste your magazine characters on this paper and name each. *On your own paper,* write approximately one page of dialogue between or among your characters.

It will add interest if there is a conflict which is resolved at the end of the story. Try to make the words sound like real people talking. Remember to put quotation marks around the exact words of any speaker and to begin a new paragraph (indent) when the speaker changes.

Refer to *MAG PICS DIALOGUE HELPER SHEET* to assist you in developing a conflict and for examples of correct use of quotation marks.

```



                    (PASTE CHARACTERS HERE)




```

Focus   *MAG PICS DIALOGUE HELPER SHEET*

Purpose: To show you how to develop a story conflict; to give examples of correct punctuation use in dialogue.

Instructions: Use this sheet to help you with *MAG PICS DIALOGUE*.

EXAMPLE OF DIALOGUE SETTING UP CONFLICT:

"It's my book!" Sandy exclaimed.

"No," replied Mark, "it does NOT belong to you."

"But . . ." Sandy was worried. She needed the book to do her homework, and now Mark said it was his.

Mark continued, "Leave me alone. It's mine and I'll prove it. What makes you think it's yours, anyway?"

Why was Mark always so sure of himself, she wondered.

HINTS ON USING QUOTATION MARKS CORRECTLY:

Line 1. Quotes around exact words Sandy says.

Line 2. Quotes around exact words Mark says. Notice commas after *no* and *Mark* to show this is an interrupted quote. Mark's exact words are *No, it does NOT belong to you.* The interrupters of his exact words are *replied Mark.*

Line 3. Quotes around exact word Sandy says. Three dots mean she doesn't finish her sentence.

Line 4. No quotes around *Mark said it was his.* This is because these are not his exact words.

Line 5. Quotes around exact words Mark says. In this case he says three sentences in a row.

Line 6. Question mark after his last remark because he asks a question. Notice the question mark comes BEFORE the quotes because it is part of his question.

Line 7. No quotes because Sandy does not say these exact words aloud.

JOKER   **FUNNY PAPERS**

Purpose: To have fun writing dialogue; to develop imagination and appreciation of humor; to develop a sense of sequence; to encourage creativity.

Save the comic sections from newspapers over a period of time. Have students bring comic books or comic sections from newspapers to class, too.

It's handy to have a large roll of butcher's paper or art planning paper on which to mount and display the students' work when completed. This makes an outstanding bulletin board!

Instructions to students: Cut out comic characters WITHOUT the printed dialogue. You can mix and match cartoon characters from different comic strips! Make up your own dialogue for a humorous sequence. You will need at least four frames, so be sure to cut out enough separate characters of the same type if they are to be in each frame. Then paste your characters in logical sequence on your paper, and add the talk balloons with your original dialogue inside them. There is no need to use quotation marks if you use balloons around the dialogue.

Variation: Artistic students can draw their own characters. By giving this additional choice, you can stimulate creativity among your students. There are usually several students in each class who prefer to create their own comic characters and have the ability to do it effectively.

Focus   *WHICH CAME FIRST—THE CHICKEN OR THE EGG?*

Name _____   Date _____

Purpose: To distinguish between cause and effect in a written explanation.

Instructions: Match the cause with the effect by connecting the lines from the causes in the first column to the logical effects in the second column.

listened to loud rock music	chicken
didn't study	got stomachache
ate too much	cat ran away
chicken	lost 3 pounds
studied hard	had to report to office
set ladder on ice	had no cavities
went on diet	received a letter
egg	fell
was late to class	lost hearing
wrote a letter to friend	passed test
forgot to feed cat	got poor grade
gave up hard candy	egg

Instructions: Complete one of the choices below.

(1) Write a paragraph of explanation beginning with one (or several) causes and leading to the logical effect or effects.

(2) Write a paragraph of explanation beginning with one (or several) effects and leading to the logical cause or causes.

Focus   *HOW DO I GET FROM HERE TO THERE?*

Purpose: To practice explaining accurately how to get from one place to another.

Instructions: Choose ONE of the following situations.

(1) Your long-forgotten cousin calls you on the telephone. He is calling from a gas station, and wants directions to get to your house. Draw a sketch of an area of town showing your neighborhood streets. Using your sketch as a guide, write a description showing your cousin exactly how to get from the gas station to your home.

(2) A new student shows up at our classroom door and asks you for directions. He needs to return two books to the library, talk to the principal in the office, and meet his friend in the lunchroom. Draw a sketch of the school floor plan, and with this as a guide, write a description showing the most efficient route for him to take.

(3) A friend of yours wants to come over to your house after his music lesson. He wants to know how to get from school to your house. Sketch a map locating your home and school. Using the sketch as a guide, write a description showing the most efficient route for him to take.

(4) The television repairman has made an appointment to check all TV sets in your house. Unfortunately, he is going to have to come while you are not home. Draw a diagram of your house floor plan. Locate all the television sets on it. Using the sketch as a guide, write a description showing the most efficient way for him to enter your house and locate all sets.

(5) You have a friend driving up to see you from over 100 miles away. He is not acquainted with the route. Draw a map to show him the way to get to your house. Using the map as a guide, write a description showing the most efficient route to get there.

(6) You are going to meet a friend from a rival school at the basketball game. He has not been to your school before. Draw a sketch of the school, showing where the gymnasium is located, and mark where you will be sitting in the gym bleachers. Using this sketch as a guide, write a description detailing how to get into the school and locate you quickly.

THIS IS HOW YOU BAKE A CAKE

Purpose: To write an explanation of how to do something; to place instructions in logical sequence.

This is how to write a how-to explanation. First, decide on your topic. Your topic is what you want to tell your readers how to do. Next, write down the steps they will need to take in order to accomplish their goal. Be sure the steps are in logical order so your explanation is easy to follow. During your writing use clue words like *first, second, next, then, lastly,* and *finally* to help your ideas flow together easily and to add clarity. Finally, end with a statement summing up the explanation. Isn't it going to be easy to write a how-to paragraph?

Instructions: Write one to three paragraphs explaining how to go about doing something. You can originate your own topic or choose one of the following:

HOW TO BAKE A CAKE (OR SOMETHING ELSE)

HOW TO MAKE LEMONADE (OR SOMETHING ELSE)

HOW TO PLAY TENNIS (OR OTHER SPORT)

HOW TO FISH (OR OTHER LEISURE-TIME PURSUIT)

HOW TO BREAK A BAD HABIT (OR FORM A GOOD HABIT)

HOW TO GIVE A SUCCESSFUL PARTY

HOW TO EARN MONEY IN YOUR SPARE TIME

HOW TO GET BETTER GRADES IN SCHOOL

HOW TO GET HAVE MORE FRIENDS

HOW TO GET ALONG WITH YOUR PARENTS

HOW TO AVOID A SUNBURN (OR OTHER PROBLEM)

HOW TO DRAW A HORSE (OR OTHER ANIMAL OR OBJECT)

HOW TO PLAY A CLARINET (OR OTHER INSTRUMENT)

HOW TO MAKE A BIRDHOUSE (OR OTHER PROJECT)

HOW TO MAKE A GOOD FIRST IMPRESSION

Focus 　　　　　　***PROVERBIAL TRUTHS***

Purpose: To learn what proverbs are; to figure out meanings of proverbs; to provide a basis for nonfiction writing.

Instructions: Choose a proverb and explain in writing what it means. If you prefer, you can make up your own proverb. One paragraph should suffice for your explanation.

HANDSOME IS AS HANDSOME DOES.

OUT OF SIGHT, OUT OF MIND.

YOU MAY DELAY, BUT TIME WILL NOT.

SPARE THE ROD AND SPOIL THE CHILD.

TALK IS CHEAP.

A WATCHED POT NEVER BOILS.

BEAUTY IS ONLY SKIN-DEEP.

HASTE MAKES WASTE.

A STITCH IN TIME SAVES NINE.

BIRDS OF A FEATHER FLOCK TOGETHER.

HE WHO LAUGHS LAST LAUGHS BEST.

A BIRD IN THE HAND IS WORTH TWO IN THE BUSH.

A PROVERB IS NO PROVERB TO YOU TILL LIFE HAS ILLUSTRATED IT.

SET THE CART BEFORE THE HORSE.

A MOB'S A MONSTER: HEADS ENOUGH, BUT NO BRAINS.

NOW IS THE TIME TO FEATHER MY NEST.

LOVE YOUR NEIGHBOR, BUT DON'T PULL DOWN YOUR HEDGE.

DON'T LEAP OUT OF THE FRYING PAN INTO THE FIRE.

BEWARE OF LITTLE EXPENSES—A SMALL LEAK WILL SINK A GREAT SHIP.

A FALSE FRIEND AND A SHADOW ATTEND ONLY WHILE THE SUN SHINES.

INTRO   TRICKY DICKY

Purpose: To trick the students; to introduce a fable where trickery is used.

Ask several trick questions or riddles:

What comes twice in every day, four times in every week, and only once in a year? Repeat the riddle a couple of times, if they ask you to. (Answer: The letter *e.*)

Which is bigger—Mrs. Bigger or Mrs. Bigger's baby? Again, repeat it, if they want to guess. (Answer: The baby is just a little Bigger.)

Point out how our minds sometimes trick us by concentrating on the wrong part of a question, issue, or story.

Read aloud the fable, "The Fox and the Crow," before assigning FABULOUS FABLES.

The Fox and the Crow

A crow who had stolen a piece of cheese was flying toward the top of a tall tree where he hoped to enjoy his prize, when a fox spied him. "If I plan this right," said the fox to himself, "I shall have cheese for supper."

So, as he sat under the tree, he began to speak in his politest tones: "Good day, mistress crow, how well you are looking today! How glossy your wings, and your breast is the breast of an eagle. And your claws—I beg pardon—your talons are as strong as steel. I have not heard your voice, but I am certain that it must surpass that of any bird just as your beauty does."

The vain crow was pleased by all the flattery. She believed every word of it and wagged her tail and flapped her wings to show her pleasure. She liked especially what friend fox said about her voice, for she had sometimes been told that her caw was a bit rusty. So, chuckling to think how she was going to surprise the fox with her most beautiful caw, she opened wide her mouth.

Down dropped the piece of cheese! The wily fox snatched it before it touched the ground, and as he walked away, licking his chops, he offered these words of advice to the silly crow: "The next time someone praises your beauty be sure to hold your tongue."

FOCUS   FABULOUS FABLES

Purpose: To become familiar with the main characteristics of a fable by going through the process of writing one; to foster creativity.

Instructions to students: Write a fable approximately one page in length. Your characters must be animals that can talk, and your fable must illustrate a lesson learned by one or more of your characters. For an introduction to teaching fables, see TRICKY DICKY.

Focus   ***I'M REALLY A PRETTY GREAT PERSON***

Name _____   **Date** _____

Purpose: To build self-image; to provide a personal writing experience.

Instructions: Fill this page by writing only good things about yourself. If you feel like writing just part of a page, you are probably overly modest or not admitting your good qualities. If you'd like to write more than a page, control yourself; we'll get the idea. Do not put your name on this paper or include it in your writing. We will try to guess who you are. If we can guess, that proves you really are a pretty great person!

FOCUS   **WRITING CONTESTS**

Purpose: To encourage polished writing; to use as an image-builder.

There are many writing contests which you can conduct or encourage students to enter. Often, just by asking, you can obtain local sponsorship from business or industry. This supplies publicity for the commercial establishment and a worthwhile prize for the winner. Well-received competitions include the following:

    ESSAY CONTEST
    POETRY CONTEST
    SCREENPLAY CONTEST
    NEWSPAPER ARTICLE CONTEST
    FICTION CONTEST
    NONFICTION CONTEST
    STORY CONTEST
    CHILDREN'S STORY CONTEST
    HUMOROUS WRITING CONTEST

Be sure all rules are specific, and announce (and post) them well ahead of time. Students MUST know what criteria will be used to judge the entries. Local businesses will allow you to post contest information even if they decide not to sponsor the contest.

FOCUS   **MOMENTOUS MILESTONES**

Purpose: To provide for a personal writing experience; to build self-image.

Instructions to students: Write about three important events in your life. Each of the three paragraphs should name one true incident and describe your feelings about it in detail.

    Examples: Birthday Party
                Acting in a Play
                Winning in a Game or Sports Event
                Divorce of Parents
                Death of Someone Close to You
                Winning an Academic Award
                Getting an Honor in Scouting
                An Unforgettable Experience

INTRO   **HAPPY HOLIDAYS**

Purpose: To prepare students before they write an explanation of an original holiday they will create.

Instructions to students: Go to the library, and read about three holidays. This will help inspire you to create a new holiday and provide background information about the history of holidays.

Follow this introductory activity with student plan sheet, *HAPPY HOLIDAYS PLAN SHEET*.

Focus   *HAPPY HOLIDAYS PLAN SHEET*

Name _____   Date _____

Purpose: To develop imagination by creating an original holiday; to write an explanation; to design a symbol to represent the holiday.

Instructions: Create a holiday you think we need, either to honor a person or notable event, or just because it would be fun. Use this plan sheet for organizing your thoughts. Then, on your own paper, write a one-page explanation of your new holiday. Design a special insignia, flag, or symbol for your holiday and include it with your paper.

NAME OF HOLIDAY_____

WHAT ARE WE CELEBRATING?_____

_____

WHY DO WE NEED IT?_____

_____

WHEN WOULD IT BE? _____

_____

HOW WOULD IT BE CELEBRATED? _____

_____

WHAT DECORATIONS WOULD BE APPROPRIATE? _____

_____

HOW IS THE HOLIDAY DIFFERENT FROM ONES WE ALREADY HAVE? _____

_____

JOKER   **ONCE UPON A TIME**

Purpose: To stimulate imagination; to have fun writing a cooperative story.

The story should be passed five or six times to make it involved and interesting. Use any easily delineated groups. In a typical class you will end up with about five stories, 3–5 minutes long, depending upon student sophistication and writing abilities. It is important that all stories be shared orally.

Instructions to students: Put your name on a sheet of paper. On the first line write, "Once upon a time," and begin to write a story. I will give you exactly one minute to write before you have to pass it on to the person next to you. That person will read silently what you have written and have one minute to continue the story in a logical way. Your stories must make sense. The last person will finish the story and not leave us dangling. After the stories are completed, we'll read them aloud and vote on which team's story we like best.

Variation: Have each student write one SENTENCE before passing it on. Increase the number of passes to ten or twelve, allowing students to have a second chance to contribute to the same story when their turns come up again.

Variation: Have each student write one sentence on the chalkboard. Call on another student to write the next, and so on. Use eight students for one story (about one-third of the class), with the last student writing a concluding sentence. Compose several stories so all students get a chance to contribute.

FOCUS   **AND THEN . . .**

Purpose: To develop imagination; to develop a sense of sequence and order of events; to give practice in drawing a conclusion.

Read aloud part of a story that is unfamiliar to the students. After characters are introduced and conflict is known, stop and say, "and then . . . you tell one more incident and resolve the conflict." For younger or slower students, say, "and then . . . you finish the story." For a sample story to read to them or to have students read to themselves, see *AND THEN . . . *

Focus   *AND THEN . .*

Purpose: To develop your imagination, sense of sequence, and the ability to draw a logical conclusion.

Instructions: Read the unfinished story. Then draw a conclusion as to what happened next. Write a logical ending. If the ending makes sense, it can be a surprise ending.

As the car sped crazily up the hill, Jeanne, her satiny blond hair falling casually over her forehead, stared intently at the loose gravel road folding up swiftly before her. As she rapidly approached the corner, she mechanically applied the brakes, but scroossh!—across the stones the car skidded until it jammed into a rut at the roadside. Thud! She felt the car tilt upside down. It was on its roof now, she thought. What will happen when it hits the side? Glass tinkled down in tiny fragments as the car hit the ground with its last, frightening jolt.

It was over. Faintly, she heard a nurse say, "You'll be all right now, child. Just get some rest so your wounds can heal."

Her body ached. Every muscle was stiff and sore. Her face itched. As she started to relieve it, her tiny hand touched gauze. She ran her fingers tentatively over the sticky bandages. Oh, how her face itched!

Then it struck her. "Wounds!" she shouted, her voice full of alarm. "Not on my face!"

"Yes," the nurse answered, "and a young man has been in several times to see you. A Richard Krr . . . Kros . . ."

"Dick! Oh yes, Dick!" Jeanne said excitedly. "But he can't see me like *this*. My face—it's—how is it, nurse?"

"A few scars, I suppose," she said. "Now, please, you must rest."

Jeanne lay back against her pillow and wondered how seriously she was hurt. True, she ached, but she expected that after being shaken around so. But her face. Scars, the nurse had said.

Thoughts were whirring in her brain. Dick had nicknamed her, "Beautiful," and now she wouldn't be. Scars. What a terrifying word! Would he still love her? Or would it be pity?

She decided. Dick wouldn't, couldn't, love her now. He was always commenting on the way she looked, admiring her smooth, tanned complexion, and saying her skin felt like he always imagined a cloud might feel. She could never let him see her looking hideous.

Three days passed. When the doctor walked in the dark room, saying "Today will tell the story," a shiver enveloped her whole body. The grey-haired nurse helped him as he unwound endless lengths of white gauze and let it pile up haphazardly on the floor. Would he *ever* finish unwrapping? Why was he going so slowly? Her heart raced; she began to tremble visibly. She grasped the mirror so tightly that her long, shapely finger nails dug their imprints into her sweating palms.

She heard Dick's voice near the doorway. Slowly he advanced toward her bed. And then . . .

(You finish the story.)

INTRO AND FOCUS   **THREE THINGS THEREIN**

Purpose: To enhance development of imagination; to introduce the writing of a logical composition or story using three unrelated words as major elements of the plot; to find unrelated nouns for use in a story.

Put the words *PERSON, PLACE,* and *OBJECT* on the chalkboard. Ask students to give you examples of people, like *boy, girl,* or *carpenter.* Do not accept proper nouns. List ten under the first category.

Then ask for specific places. Examples: (*school, cave, park*). List ten under this second category.

Finally, ask for unrelated objects, such as *necklace, dictionary,* and *hammer.* List these under the third category. Do NOT tell students why you are asking for these words, or it will spoil the surprise.

(If you prefer to embark on the assignment without drawing ideas through class discussion, use prepared sheet, *MAKE A CONNECTION*). Otherwise, use instructions below.

Instructions to students: Write a story using three words directly across from each other on the chalkboard. Make a logical connection among the three words, and be sure they play important roles in your writing. Underline the unrelated nouns.

Focus   *MAKE A CONNECTION*

Purpose: To develop your imagination and creativity; to write a story.

Instructions: Write a story using any three words in the rows below. (Rows go from left to right.) The words are basically unrelated.

The tricks are to make a logical connection among the words and to use the trio of words as important, necessary parts of your story. In your story, underline the three unrelated words you choose. Be sure your story has a problem that is worked out at the end.

PERSON	PLACE	THING
carpenter	opera house	necklace
milkman	bank	rubber ducky
mailman	city dump	lamp
sausage-maker	park	glasses
teacher	factory	animal crackers
jockey	television studio	house
thief	fire station	dictionary
grandmother	police station	hammer
fur trader	school	picture
bank robber	swimming pool	typewriter
baby	gymnasium	computer
teenager	funeral parlor	paper clip
welder	dance	file cabinet
mechanic	laundromat	canoe paddle
rock star	library	stop sign

When you are finished, we'll read some of the stories aloud in class.

INTRO   **I DIDN'T KNOW THAT!**

Purpose: To give practice in note-taking; to provide social interaction among peers; to develop interviewing skills; to provide a basis for a written composition.

Pair your students. You can use a numbering system where every student says a consecutive number. Designate the pairs randomly such as 1 and 13, 2 and 24. Students feel this is fair, and this system avoids friends interviewing friends they already know well. (The fun and interviewing skill goes out of the activity if students already know the answers!)

Discuss possibilities of questions to ask the interviewee:

Age

Family

Size Placement in Family (Oldest, Youngest, Middle)

Hobbies

Favorites (Music, Sports)

Unusual Things That Have Happened to Them

Other Schools Attended

Pet Peeves

Elicit ideas from the class, and write them on the chalkboard as reminders, or use the reproducible handout, *I DIDN'T KNOW THAT*.

Depending on the writing abilities of the students and class time available, this lesson may take from one to three class sessions. If you want a more polished writing, insist on proofreading and revision.

I DIDN'T KNOW THAT!

Purpose: To give practice in note-taking; to develop interviewing skills; to provide a basis for a written composition.

Instructions: You are going to interview a partner to try to find out interesting and different things about him that the rest of the class does not know. You will be taking notes as the interview progresses and writing your composition after you gather the needed information.

You will have ten minutes to write on your paper at least six questions to ask your partner. Be sure the questions are open-ended. Ask questions that cannot be answered by a simple YES or NO, but ones which encourage interesting and unique responses. After each question, leave a few blank lines for your notes.

Your questions can include family size, placement in family (oldest, youngest, middle), hobbies, favorite things (music, sports, etc.), unusual things that have happened to him, or other special questions you decide to ask. Try not to insult your partner by asking anything offensive or overly personal.

I will tell you when to begin interviewing, and give you fifteen minutes. As you interview, take notes. Be sure to be accurate and complete with your notes because you will not be able to go back to your partner to fill in extra information you may have missed or forgotten to jot down.

When your fifteen minutes are up, I'll signal you to switch from interviewer to interviewee. Your partner will interview you in the same way you questioned him, again having fifteen minutes to complete his notes. I will let you know when the note-taking time is up. At that time, separate yourselves from your partner and begin your composition. Remember, you cannot contact your partner during your writing phase of this project.

Try to tell your partner something special. See if you can make him say, "I didn't know that!"

FOCUS   **DAILY JOURNALS**

Purpose: To encourage habitual expression of thoughts in writing; to provide for therapeutic release of feelings; to collect individual writings over a period of time in one notebook.

A journal is a notebook or other semi-permanent container housing the writings of one student. Writing in journals over a period of time provides students with a collection of writings, and can serve as a productive emotional outlet. One compelling way to learn to write is by writing often and regularly. Requiring students to write in journals every day is a powerful technique.

You can assign varied types of writing for different writing sessions:

explanation
description
story
poetry
observation
personal experience
fable
paragraph
report
letters

Or, **you** can assign specific topics revolving around personal experiences and feelings:

My Most Embarrassing Moment
What I'd Like to Change About School
My Most Exciting Experience
My Best Friend
A Plan for an Ideal Day
How Kids Con Parents
My Most Upsetting Experience
The Best Thing That Ever Happened to Me
An Honor or Award I Received
What Makes Me Mad
What Makes Me Nervous

Another possibility is to assign a timed writing period every day, but allow complete freedom for the student to express himself in any way and on any topic he chooses.

You may prefer to combine parts of each of these alternatives, sometimes assigning, sometimes allowing free expression. You may decide on weekly or semi-weekly journal entries, rather than daily writing.

FOCUS   **COOPERATIVE JOURNAL ENTRIES**

Purpose: To provide a basis for journal entries; to develop library and research skills; to provide peer interaction toward a common goal; to develop skills in presenting a report.

Divide the class into groups of four or five. Assign each group a part of a larger research project. For example, if pilgrims are their overall topic, one group might research why the pilgrims left England; another group, the journey to America; a third group, arriving and setting up their community; and the last group, the first Thanksgiving.

After each group gives its oral presentation to the class on their portion of the project, every student writes a first person narrative (in this example, from a pilgrim's point of view) as his journal entry. In the pilgrim example, each student writes four journal entries as if he were living and participating in the events of the historical period being studied.

INTRO   ENVELOPE ENIGMA

Purpose: To stimulate interest in envelopes; to introduce a lesson on correct ways to fold business and friendly letters, insert them into envelopes, and address envelopes properly.

Before students arrive draw an envelope outline as shown below. Instruct them to draw the envelope outline with one continuous line. The challenge is they cannot go over any line a second time, nor lift their pens or pencils from their papers.

The first student to do it correctly can illustrate his solution on the chalkboard. If another student has a different explanation, he should also demonstrate his solution.

Harder Variation: Don't retrace a line; don't lift pen; AND don't cross any line.

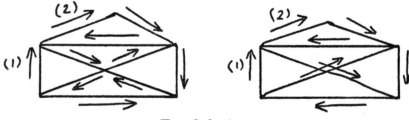

Two Solutions

Name _____   Date _____

Purpose: To write a real, rather than make-believe, letter.

Riddle: Is it safe to write a letter on any empty stomach?

Riddle Answer: _____

Instructions: Please complete one of the following assignments.

(1) Write a real letter to a friend or relative. It must be a minimum of one page on one side, but may be longer. Write the first draft in class, and submit it to me for corrections and suggestions. (I will keep the contents confidential.)

When the letter is returned to you, rewrite it on suitable stationery. Fold the letter properly, insert in a correctly addressed, stamped envelope, and *without sealing it,* hand it in to me again. I will evaluate it (not making any marks or comments on your letter), seal it, and mail it for you.

(2) Write a real business letter to a company or business. It must be a minimum of one-half page on one side. Be sure to use correct business letter format and punctuation. The rest of the instructions are the same as (1) above.

(3) Write a real invitation to someone to visit the classroom, your home, a party, or other function. The rest of the instructions remain the same as (1) above.

(4) Write a real thank-you note to someone who has done something nice for you (visited you, given you a gift, helped you out in some way). The rest of the instructions are the same as (1) above.

Riddle: What begins with P, ends with E, and has thousands of letters?

Riddle Answer: _____

When everyone has completed the assignment, we'll share possible riddle answers. You may have more clever answers than the originals!

INTRO AND FOCUS   V.I.P. VISITOR

Purpose: To present a need to write actual invitations and thank-you notes; to build self-esteem.

Have students invite someone to visit the class (perhaps the principal, another teacher, a parent, or someone from the community). Each student should write an invitation to the person he would like to invite. As a group they can decide who would be most interesting to actually invite, and who should be designated to copy one of the invitations on proper stationery.

Appoint a welcomer to meet the person and an introducer to introduce the visitor to the class. (These are the esteem-builders.)

Follow up this activity with each student writing a thank-you note to the visitor and actually mailing the notes.

INTRO AND FOCUS   MAGNIFICENT MAGNIFICATION

Purpose: To gain skill in observing; to arouse curiosity; to give written practice in describing accurately what is seen; to provide practice in deductive reasoning.

Put a tiny, unusual object in a closed, glass jar on your desk. Place a magnifying glass next to the jar for student use. You can ferret out small, thought-provoking items from shops that carry hardware, electronics, or hobby and crafts articles. A well-stocked (especially older) fishing tackle box or sewing basket also often yields objects of interest.

Instructions to students: Write a one-paragraph description of what the object looks like, what it might be used for, and what you think it is. Give it a name. Be sure to describe the color, texture, shape, material, and possible use.

INTRO   PUT ME IN THE MOOD

Purpose: To provide practice in deliberately creating a mood through the author technique of sound repetition.

Put examples on the chalkboard (or read examples) of poetry or prose which create definite moods through sound repetition. Hand out the student worksheet, *PUT ME IN THE MOOD*, for a follow-up assignment.

PUT ME IN THE MOOD

Purpose: To provide practice in deliberately creating mood through the author technique of sound repetition.

A mood is a state of mind, attitude, feeling, or disposition. Writers often use sound repetition to create moods for readers.

Instructions: Write a paragraph intentionally creating a mood by repeating sounds. Try to create the feeling, not necessarily to tell a story. (A short description is one way.)

Choose one of the following moods, or combine other sounds you feel create a definite mood. Title your paragraph with the mood you are trying to create.

- Create a mood of gloom and mystery by repeating double *o* sounds (*oo*—as in gloom) in a short piece of creative description. Hint to begin: The gloomy room . . .

- Create a mood of sadness and slowness by repeating long vowel sounds (*a, e, i. o, u*) in a short piece of creative description. Example: She used her eyes to plead.

- Create a mood of lightness and speed by repeating short vowel sounds (*a, e, i, o, u*) in a short piece of creative description. Example: Deftly, quickly, he did his job.

- Create a mood of harshness by repeating hard consonants (*b, g, c, d, k, p, t*), in a short piece of creative description. Example: Beat, drums, beat!

- Create a mood of repulsion by repeating the *s* sound in a short piece of creative description. Hint to begin: The slithering, slimy snake . . .

- Create a mood of your choice by using sound repetitions.

When most of you are finished, we will share the paragraphs orally without revealing what mood you are trying to create. We will try to see if you have succeeded in putting us IN THE MOOD!

FOCUS   **NEWSPAPER KNOWLEDGE**

Purpose: To learn how to find answers to everyday questions in a newspaper; to discover where to locate needed information quickly.

Accumulate and distribute newspapers to students. You can use large, small, local, out-of-town, current, or older papers. Diversity is advantageous. Preferably, have one complete newspaper for each student. If this isn't possible, have at least one complete newspaper for every pair of students.

Set up a series of situations and questions so students can ferret out answers. Example:

You want to go to a flea market. What days are they open? What hours will each be open? Which ones are going to be available at times suitable to you? Where is each located? Are directions given for getting there? What are the special items, if any, that are being advertised?

For a set of situations and questions pertaining to each, see *NEWSPAPER KNOWLEDGE*.

INTRO   **NEWS HOUND**

Purpose: To build self-image; to learn to work cooperatively; to understand different types of writing found in newspapers.

Distribute newspapers of students. Discuss the main types of newspaper articles: human interest (feature) stories, editorials (columns), current ("hard") news, sports news, general information, and social events. Follow with CLASSY NEWSPAPER.

Instructions to students: Find examples of each type and cut them out of the papers. Then put all the articles of the same type together in Manila folders. As a class you will have six folders, one for each category.

Purpose: To learn how to find answers to everyday questions in a newspaper; to discover where to locate needed information quickly.

Instructions: Ferret out answers to the following situations by looking in the newspaper. Number the situation, and clearly show which question you are answering. Use your own paper.

> EXAMPLE: 1. Show Playing—"Fugitive"
>   When—Feb. 10-Feb. 14; 8:15-10:15 p.m.
>   Where—Taylor Theatre
>   Front Street
>   Taylor, Ohio
>   Price—$2.50 adults
> $2.00 children 12 and under
>   Stars—Michael J. Fox
>   Vanessa Redgrave
>   Plot—Unknown (newspaper does not say)

1. You want to go to the show. What is playing? When does it begin and end (times and dates)? Where is it playing (theater, location)? How much will it cost you? Who are the actors and actresses? Do you know what it is about?

2. You want to put your summer earnings in the bank. What banks are available? What is the interest rate at each? Where are they located (address, town)? What are their phone numbers? Do they advertise any special services to make you want to deposit your earnings there?

3. You want to buy some new clothes. What stores are available? Where are they located? Do any of the stores have sales? What is the name of their sale (or why are they having a sale)? How much are the markdowns? When does the sale begin and end? What hours are the stores open?

4. You like single-pane cartoons. How many of these one-frame jokes are in your newspaper? Who are the humorists? What are the names of the cartoons? Describe a single-pane cartoon from the paper, and tell why you think it's funny.

5. You wanted to go on a picnic on the same day your newspaper was published. What was the date? What was the weather like on that day? Would it have been better or worse if you had gone the next day? Where did the weather report show the warmest weather? The coldest? The rainiest?

6. You want to know how a sports event turned out. List one event. When and where did it take place? Who were the rival teams? Who won? What was the score? Who was a starring player?

FOCUS   **CLASSY NEWSPAPER**

Purpose: To give practice in writing nonfiction; to learn to work well with others; to understand different types of writing found in newspapers; to build self-image. For introductory activity, see NEWS HOUND.

Discuss briefly the duties of editor, copy editor, proofreader, lay-out editor, printer, writer, advertising editor, sales personnel, and art and photography editor. Have the students elect interested classmates to fulfill these roles.

You may want to have co-editors, as well as several proofreaders, "printers," and salespeople. Partnerships work well for certain students; single jobs are best for others. Try to include at least one article from each student in the final publication.

This activity will take several weeks to complete. If students enjoy it and are productive, you may want to put out additional issues of the class newspaper during the year. In schools where permitted, students can sell papers for a nominal fee to earn money for a needed room item. See *CLASSY NEWSPAPER* for handout for students.

JOKER   **OBSERVATION TREPIDATION**

Purpose: To develop observation skills; to develop memory recall; to have fun while thinking and concentrating.

Lay out ten known objects (this is not a guessing game). Give the students a designated amount of time to observe the objects. Cover or put away the items, and have each student make a list of as many as he can remember. You can experiment with this during the year, using different objects and/or a larger number of items as students become more proficient. If you are working with very slow students, fewer objects would be appropriate.

CLASSY NEWSPAPER

Purpose: To help you understand various newspaper jobs so you can decide how you'd like to participate in a class newspaper; to practice writing nonfiction articles; to learn to cooperate with others.

Editor (oversee paper and decide what to include)

Copy Editor (make minor changes and corrections)

Proofreader (proofread final copy before printing)

Lay-out Editor (decide what goes where)

"Printer" (type, word-process, or print articles onto the paper and duplicate needed copies)

Reporter (write articles for newspaper)

Advertising Editor (oversee ads in paper)

Sales Personnel (organize the selling of papers)

Art and Photography Editor (oversee artwork and photography, if any)

Instructions to students: Look over the job descriptions of people needed to put out a class newspaper. See which ones interest you and for which you feel qualified. We will vote on students to fill each job after we discuss the positions.

Write two articles to submit to the editors for your class newspaper. Articles must be of two different types. (For example, you can't write two sports articles; one must be from another category.)

Look through the Manila folders for examples of articles to use as models. Remember the basic types are human interest (feature) stories, editorials and columns, current "hard" news, sports news, general information, and social events. You may also write (or draw) an advertisement to substitute for one of your required articles.

Submit articles to the editor as soon as you are finished. (Ads should be given to the advertising editor.) If the editor feels your article needs major revisions, I will work with you to improve it. Use any extra time to help others as needed.

INTRO AND FOCUS   **MONKEY DO; MONKEY WRITE**

Purpose: To increase powers of observation; to provide practice in taking notes in sequence; to use notes to help recall details; to write an accurate description of what took place.

Instructions to students: I am going to perform a series of actions. I want you to watch me carefully and take accurate notes telling what you observe. Keep your notes in proper sequence. After I finish, you will have to rely on your powers of observation and note-taking to write a one-paragraph description of the actions which took place. You will be able to use your notes while you write, but cannot compare notes with anyone else in the class.

You (or a student) perform a series of ten actions or activities in front of the class. The actions might include (1) erasing the chalkboard, (2) coughing, (3) picking up a piece of paper from the floor, (4) playing patty-cake with the chalkboard, (5) touching a particular student on the shoulder, (6) getting a book off the shelves, (7) blowing your nose with a tissue, (8) closing the door, (9) sitting down, and (10) reading a book.

Try to work in the coughing and nose-blowing as incidentally as possible to be sure they are observing carefully. Do NOT tell them how many actions you are doing.

INTRO   **DEVIL'S ADVOCATE**

Purpose: To stimulate students to think of reasons in defense of their opinions; to provide a nonfiction writing assignment emphasizing topic sentence, details to support an opinion, and clincher sentence.

Confront students with several opinions you are reasonably sure are in conflict with their own. Continue by presenting reasons you feel the way you do. (You need not believe in the position you are advocating, but be convincing in your arguments.) For handout of topics which bring controversy (sometimes vehement objections!), see *DEFEND YOURSELF*.

Focus   ***DEFEND YOURSELF***

Purpose: To practice writing using a topic sentence, details to support an opinion, and clincher sentence.

Instructions: Choose one of the following topics and write a rebuttal on the subject. Be sure you have a topic sentence (you can revise a sentence below), at least three logical reasons to support your opinion, and a clincher sentence. If you prefer to defend your opinion on a different subject, see me.

(1) People should not be allowed to obtain a driver's license until they are 21 years old. The main reason is that young drivers cause the most accidents. If the young drivers were off the road, we could save lives. They are immature and show it by putting their arms around their girlfriends and drinking alcohol while driving. They also like to burn rubber skidding around corners. Some are even too short to see over the steering wheel! Most youngsters can't afford to drive, anyway. It costs money for gasoline, oil, and repairs. Why should parents have to pay for all this? These are the reasons I think people should reach the age of majority before driving.

(2) Students should not watch television on school nights. First, they get so engrossed in make-believe, they find it difficult to turn their attention to the real world of homework. Homework can seem dull after the exciting episodes they see. Second, they waste all their time, and there is none left for school work or sleep. Finally, TV is hard on their eyes. The constant blinking of the set and staring into a bright, white screen tire their eyes and make them red. Students don't feel like reading after watching the tube. So ban the boob tube on school nights!

(3) Boy-girl parties should be reserved for high school students. Elementary and middle school students don't know how to act with the opposite sex. They giggle and horse around all the time. The boys are too shy to ask the girls to dance, and the girls don't ask the boys because the boys are too short for them. Another reason is that when boys and girls get too interested in each other when they are young, they tend to think only of each other. They forget about their schoolwork, their other friends, their families, and their responsibilities. I think it is better to save mixed parties for later on when people are in high school.

(4) We should have school all year. We are bound to learn more in twelve months than in nine. Also, we forget half of what we did learn when we take three months off for vacation. (It's hard to remember things when you don't use them.) I think parents would like year-round school because they wouldn't have to hire a babysitter in the summer. This would save them money, and they would know we were doing something worthwhile. Teachers would like it, too. They would get paid higher salaries and wouldn't need to work extra during June, July, and August. Maybe if teachers were paid more, we'd get more qualified teachers, and that would benefit us as well. Yes, having school all year is better for everybody.

JOKER   *SCRAMBLED EGGS*

Name _____   Date _____

Purpose: To have fun with outlines; to clinch an understanding of the hierarchy of outlining.

Instructions: The following eggs are scrambled. Restructure the outline so that main
ideas are represented by Roman numerals, and supporting ideas are represented by *A, B, C,*
or *D.* You will *not* need to make any changes in the NUMERALS or LETTERS representing topics and subtopics. Unscramble only the words and phrases. Put your unscrambled
eggs on the right side of this sheet.

EGGS   EGGS

I. White   I. _____

   A. Brown   A. _____

   B. Boiled   B. _____

   C. High cholesterol   C. _____

   D. Ways to prepare   D. _____

II. Colors   II. _____

   A. Low calories   A. _____

   B. Poached   B. _____

III. Advantages   III. _____

   A. Fried   A. _____

   B. High protein   B. _____

   C. Disadvantages   C. _____

IV. Inexpensive   IV. _____

   A. Scrambled   A. _____

   B. Allergenic   B. _____

INTRO   **ILLEGIBILITY**

Purpose: To arouse interest in good penmanship; to show the necessity of good handwriting for accurate written communication; to introduce a lesson on penmanship.

Before students enter the room, write a completely illegible sentence on the chalkboard. If you find this difficult, practice until you get effective ones; then put them on an overhead transparency so you have them in permanent form. The image should be showing on the screen or chalkboard as students enter the room. This will definitely arouse interest!

With perseverance, a few students should be able to figure out the message. Be sure the message is important or interesting to the students, or they won't bother trying to work on it. Examples:

Recess at twelve!   No homework tonight!

Go to the library now.

This attention-getter is effective even if used as often as twice a month. If used more than that, it gets tiresome. It keeps students focused on the importance of good handwriting by involving them in trying to decipher a message they sincerely WANT to read, but have difficulty in understanding because of poor penmanship. It reminds them in graphic fashion that when penmanship is illegible, messages can be misread or not understood at all.

INTRO   **PENMANSSSSSHIP**

Purpose: To attract visual attention to the main aspects of good penmanship; to visually show both good and poor examples of handwriting.

Write out examples of slant, size, shape, spacing, and sightline, discussing each. If you are not adept at this on a spontaneous basis, make a reproducible copy for each student. For a time-saver, see *PENMANSSSSSHIP*.

You should show mixed slant, backhand, straight up-and-down, and correct slant. Demonstrate proper size, overly large, immature writing, and hard-to-read, tiny writing. Emphasize correct ways to form various letters and how to space evenly between letters. Finally, show how superior penmanship requires aiming for the sightline and hitting the target with the appropriate part of the letter.

Focus   *PENMANSSSSSHIP*

Name _____   **Date** _____

Purpose: To show the five major features of good handwriting; to provide practice in each.

SLANT should be consistent.   *This slant goes*

This slant goes every which way.

Mary Jordan

This handwriting slants to the left.

This has no slant.

This handwriting has no slant.

BEST *This is the best slant.*

This slant is the most ideal.

SIZE should be reasonable.   *This is too small.*

This handwriting is too small.

This is too large.

This handwriting is too large.

BEST *This is about right.*

This handwriting is the right size.

SHAPE should be proper.   *These letters are not*

These letters are not shaped properly.

BEST *These letters are proper.*

These letters are shaped properly.

Focus   *PENMANSSSSSHIP* (continued)

SPACING should be even.   *Uneven spacing*
This handwriting is spaced unevenly!

                    BEST *even spacing*
This handwriting is spaced evenly.

SIGHTLINE should be hit.   *Ooops – missed*
This writing shows sightline missed.

                    BEST *base sightline hit*
This writing shows sightline hit.

Instructions: Practice your five *S's* on these lines. Be consistent and legible. Write **part of** the following sentence on each line. (It uses all the letters of the alphabet.)

THE QUICK, BROWN FOX JUMPED OVER THE LAZY DOGS.

_____
Slant

_____
Size

_____
Shape

_____
Spacing

_____
Sightline

Focus   ***LIKE-DISLIKE***

Purpose: To practice writing a nonfiction account, expressing your feelings about a subject.

Instructions: I am interested in your viewpoint and ideas. Choose one topic, and develop three major aspects of the topic into a well-organized, one-page composition.

WHAT I LIKE (DISLIKE) ABOUT ADULTS

WHAT I LIKE (DISLIKE) ABOUT A PARTICULAR ADULT

WHAT I LIKE (DISLIKE) ABOUT SCHOOL

WHAT I LIKE (DISLIKE) ABOUT MY FAMILY

WHAT I LIKE (DISLIKE) ABOUT MYSELF

WHAT I LIKE (DISLIKE) ABOUT MY LIFE

WHAT I LIKE (DISLIKE) ABOUT MY FRIEND (OR FRIENDS)

MY FAVORITE (LEAST FAVORITE) THINGS TO DO

WHY I LIKE (DISLIKE) SPRING (FALL, SUMMER, WINTER)

MY FAVORITE (LEAST FAVORITE) BOOK

MY FAVORITE (LEAST FAVORITE) MOVIE

MY FAVORITE (LEAST FAVORITE) MOVIE ACTOR (ACTRESS)

MY FAVORITE (LEAST FAVORITE) TELEVISION SHOW

MY BEST (WORST) VACATION

MY FAVORITE (LEAST FAVORITE) FOODS

Purpose: To practice writing a nonfiction account, expressing your feelings about yourself

Instructions: I am interested in understanding your viewpoint and ideas. Choose one starter sentence and write as truthfully as you can. One page on one side should be adequate.

SOMETIMES I . . .

I NEVER . . .

I ALWAYS . . .

I AM BEST AT . . .

I AM WORST AT . . .

I WISH . . .

IF I COULD ONLY . . .

WHEN I GET OLDER, I . . .

IF I HAD MY WAY, I'D . . .

I AM THE KIND OF PERSON WHO . . .

I DREAM OF SOMEDAY . . .

I WANT TO . . .

I NEVER WANT TO . . .

I USUALLY . . .

JOKER   **LIMERICKING AROUND THE ROOM**

Purpose: To build self-image by displaying student work; to challenge students to write so many limericks that they will circle completely around the room on all four walls; to provide a culminating activity after composing limericks.

Have students print original limericks on 4″ × 6″, unlined note cards with various colors of medium-point felt pens. Each child should have at least one limerick displayed. Your poetic students will be more prolific.

Tear off 2″–3″ strips of masking tape, and double the strips around your finger into small circles (sticky side out) to attach note cards to walls of classroom. This won't leave any scars on the walls. Students enjoy sticking up their own limericks. If you put some up straight, some catty-corner left, some catty-corner right, and even a few upside down, the display will be in character with the light-hearted poetry. Students will amuse themselves before, during, and after class reading them until you have indeed "limericked around the room" successfully.

Variation: Poetry in couplets or haiku form also provides an easy-to-write vehicle for successful "around the room" display.

INTRO   **NAME RIDDLE**

Purpose: To gain attention before using students' names in poetry writing.

Riddle: What is yours, but your friends use more than you do?
(Wait for guesses.)
Answer: Your name.
See NAME THAT POEM and *NAME THAT POEM* for follow-up activity.

FOCUS   **NAME THAT POEM**

Purpose: To ensure personal involvement while creating a poem by using their names as a starting point.

Have students print their names vertically on their papers, one letter to a line. If students are older and more familiar with poetry, have them use their complete first and last names. Younger students can use nicknames, which tend to be shorter.

Students write poetry using these letters to begin each line.

Variation: If you are studying a particular type of poetry, such as couplet, haiku, lyric, limerick, or narrative, adjust the number of lines to suit by adding arbitrary letters or subtracting letters. Examples:

Limit the name to the five first letters if you are
      emphasizing limericks.
Use initials for couplets.
If the name is too short, you could add letters from the
      last name.

Joker   ***NAME THAT POEM***

Name _____   Date _____

Purpose: To have fun while writing a poem.

Riddle: What is yours, but your friends use more than you do?

Answer: _____

Instructions: Print your name vertically on your paper, using one line for each letter. Use your first full name, not your nickname, unless the teacher tells you otherwise.

Write a poem, rhyming or not, humorous or serious, using the letter of your name to begin each word in the new line. Wait for any special instructions before you begin writing (in case the teacher wants you to write a specific type of poem you have been studying).

Example:

B ill, Bill, that's my name.
I always like to play a game.
L et me know when you begin.
L ists and things I always win.
Y es, I am a boy of fame!

Practice writing your poem on scrap paper. Put the final version neatly on the lines below.

INTRO AND FOCUS   **LYRIC POEM**

Purpose: To express emotions in poetic form; to learn about and understand what a lyric poem is.

Explain that everyone has emotions; they are how we feel; we need not be ashamed or embarrassed by our emotions. Mention that many popular songs are composed of lyrics or words that express feelings. Point out that some emotions are transitory; others are more permanent.

Ask students to think back in time to emotions they have experienced. List their examples on the chalkboard and discuss. You can suggest emotions to write about that students may not mention during the discussion: sadness, joy, pride, excitement, disappointment, love, hatred, frustration, fear. Students should not feel limited to the possibilities listed on the chalkboard.

Read a lyric poem for them or play a recording or tape of an emotional popular song as a model. Probably the latter will be more enthusiastically received! You may want to read a lyric poem with mood music in the background to provide an example of what your assignment will entail. (If you are poetic, students will be favorably impressed if you "bare your soul" a bit with a lyric poem you have written. This helps to set the stage for them to be more free to do the same.)

When you make the assignment which follows, place no restrictions on their lyric poem length, rhyme (or lack of it), or meter, but discuss the differences between poetry and prose. Be sure they recognize that poetry is usually more emotional, flowing, and rhythmical.

Instructions to student: Compose a poem that shows emotion. It should show how you feel now or how you felt at some previous time. Choose a musical tape or record that reflects a similar mood or feeling. Read your poem to the class with your selected music. You can use the music as background while you are reading or play it for the class separately. Instrumental music usually provides appropriate background; vocal renditions usually need to be played separately.

Variation: Have students pick a lyric poem someone else has written and put suitable musical background to it for reading to the class. (This variation could involve going to the library to seek poetry from collections, and finding the music and rehearsing for reading the poem to the class as a homework assignment.)

Variation: Use *LYRIC POEM READING* student worksheet.

Name _____   **Date** _____

Purpose: To express emotions in poetic form; to learn about and understand what a lyric poem is.

Everyone has emotions; they are how we feel; we need not be ashamed or embarrassed by our emotions. Many popular songs are composed of lyrics or words that express feelings. Some feelings are transitory; others are more permanent.

Instructions: Think back in time to emotions you have experienced. List several examples of emotions you have felt.

FLEETING FEELINGS   _____

                           _____

LASTING FEELINGS   _____

                           _____

Choose one of the emotions you listed, and compose a poem that expresses these feelings. The lyric poem should show how you feel right now or how you felt at some previous time.

Then think of a musical tape or record that reflects a similar mood or feeling. (You may choose the music in your mind first, and use it as inspiration for your poem.) You will be reading your poem to the class with your selected musical background. You can play the music softly as you read, or play it before or after reading your poem. (Instrumentals usually provide appropriate background; vocal renditions usually need to be played separately.)

Use the space below to help in planning your presentation.

MUSIC: Title _____

   Why I Am Choosing It _____

MY POEM: Title _____

   Emotion I Am Trying to Express _____

   Specific Words, Sounds, or Phrases That Help Create the Mood

_____

_____

INTRO   **MUSICAL MOTIF**

Purpose: To use music to provide inspiration or a theme for creative writing, either poetry or prose.

Choose a recording or tape that has varied rhythms and colorful themes. If the music is not of the rousing variety, you may wish to dim (not darken) the room during the musical interlude. You can play as much of a selection as you wish, but less than ten minutes is a good guide time. This way students do not get restless, and there is ample time to develop their compositions. See *WRITING TO RHYTHM* for follow-up activity.

The following music supplies inspiration and brings forth varied writing from students:

"Pictures at an Exhibition"—Moussorgsky
"New World Sympony"—Dvorak
"The Nutcracker Suite"—Tchaikovsky
"Liebestraum"—Liszt
"Military Suite in F"—Holst
"Tales from the Vienna Woods"—Strauss
"Seventeen Come Sunday"—Williams
"Peer Gynt Suite"—Grieg
"William Tell Overture"—Rossini
"Peter and the Wolf"— Prokofiev
"Appalachian Suite"—Copeland
"Dance of the Clowns"—Mendelssohn
"Flight of the Bumble Bee"—Rimsky-Korsakov

JOKER   **MUFFED UP—WHAT NOW?**

Purpose: To show the necessity of proofreading and rewriting by using personal involvement.

Transfer errors from students' writing assignments onto an overhead transparency. Copy the words and mistakes exactly as the students have written them, with the title MUFFED UP—WHAT NOW? Have the transparency projected as

Name _____   **Date** _____

Purpose: To have fun while polishing proofreading skills.

Instructions: Test your proofreading skills! There is at least one error in each of the following sentences. A change, addition, or deletion of one ingredient (letter) will make an improvement in the pudding. Make the corrections on this sheet.

1. John and Mary are brother and mister.

2   They have three pet logs which they glove yearly.

3. John calls one dog Spot because he has several spats on his back.

4. Another he calls Plackie because of his bark color.

5. The pig dog is Mary's favorite.

6. One day the lids and all the hogs went on a bike to the woods.

7. They saw the squirrels gun, the rabbits mop, and the nirds fly.

8. When they got hope, they decided to rake some pudding.

9. John panted to make chocolate, but Mary preferred mustard.

10. Finally, they agreed to fake a catch of utterscotch.

Focus

WRITING TO RHYTHM

Purpose: To enhance creativity and provide inspiration for writing.

Instructions: Listen carefully and quietly to the entire piece of music. You may take notes or draw pictures on this sheet while the music is playing. Your notes and drawings should show how the music makes you feel or what certain parts of the music remind you of.

Try to relax and put yourself in a dreamy state of mind, receptive to the music and your feelings. At the end of the musical interlude write a poem or narrative that relates to what you heard. Do not begin writing until the music stops.

If you think it would be helpful, I can repeat the music very softly while you are writing. This may help to reaffirm your impressions and create further inspiration.

USE THE SPACE BELOW FOR NOTES, DRAWINGS, AND FEELINGS. (You will write your actual poem or narrative on a separate piece of paper.)

students enter the room. They are extremely interested in seeing if any of their work is projected. This technique is effective any time you discuss rewriting or proofreading, not just the first time the concepts are broached.

Go over each excerpt, extracting from students any corrections and suggestions for improvement. You should not identify the individuals whose mistakes were chosen, but often they will reveal themselves to the class because they enjoy the recognition.

The students who made the errors benefit by having suggestions and corrections made. For the students who make the suggestions and corrections, the exercise acts as an image-builder. Students who are not directly involved benefit because they are alerted to problems which they should avoid in future writing.

FOCUS   RANDOM REPORTS

Purpose: To give practice in note-taking and writing an informational narrative report.

Before the class enters the room, place one encyclopedia volume and three $4'' \times 6''$, lined note cards on the desk of each student. (Have some extra note cards handy in case they are needed.) Be sure the encyclopedia chosen is at a reasonable reading level for your students.

Instructions to students: Browse through your volume of the encyclopedia until you find a topic of interest. You may not trade volumes with anyone else.

Use your cards on one side only to take notes on unusual or fascinating information you would like to share with the class. Do NOT use complete sentences; pick key words and main ideas. I will be checking your note cards before you begin writing your report to help you with any difficulties. Prepare to read your report to the class.

Variation: Students can use their notes to report orally.

INTRO   OCCUPATIONS OCTOPUS

Purpose: To introduce a lesson in library research skills (finding information and note-taking) and report-writing; to pique curiosity about an upcoming assignment.

You will need to supply $4'' \times 6''$, lined note cards for their note-taking. You will also need varied colors of standard construction paper, scissors, and felt pens.

Focus   ***OCCUPATIONS OCTOPUS***

Purpose: To develop library research skills (finding information and note-taking); to practice report-writing; to use an occupation as the topic of study.

Instructions: Each of you will explore one occupation. It can be the present or former occupation of one of your parents or guardians, or another occupation that interests you.

First, cut out of colored construction paper a facsimile of an octopus leg about 15″ long and 2″ wide. On it PRINT in felt pen the name of the occupation you are going to research. Be sure to spell it correctly. You can then add your leg to the octopus body on the bulletin board.

Next, take seven note cards and label each with one of the following headings:

Training
Duties
Salary Range
Advancement Possibilities
Advantages
Disadvantages
Why I Would (or Wouldn't) Like It

As you read about these topics, take notes on the appropriate card.

Places to look for occupational information:

Vertical file in the school or public library
Guidance counselor (interview)
Guidance counselor's library of occupational materials
Encyclopedia
Library books (nonfiction section; use
    card catalog)
Parents or guardians (interview)

After you have found enough information on your occupation, use your notes to write a report. Organize the report in the same order that the note cards are listed above.

Several days before their assignment (*OCCUPATIONS OCTOPUS*), make the nucleus of the body of an octopus, and display it on the bulletin board. It should have no label. Encourage curious students to guess what it is, but don't tell them what it represents. Indicate they will find out shortly when they help you complete it. This will serve to advertise their upcoming project and stimulate interest. For a reproducible handout of assignment to follow see *OCCUPATIONS OCTOPUS*.

INTRO AND FOCUS   TUNING UP YOUR SENSES

Purpose: To enhance development of the five senses; to provide a descriptive writing experience.

Bring in six unusual, hard-to-distinguish objects. Put them in a gunny sack or pillow case. A student comes up, reaches in, and touches an object. He can examine it with the senses of touch and hearing only. He cannot remove it from the sack to see it, taste it, or smell it. Provocative objects are velvet or silk fabric; woodcarving; an unusual ceramic shape; an obscure fruit or vegetable; kapok or pillow stuffing; an uncommon metal tool.

Instructions to students: Write a short description of each article from memory, emphasizing how it felt and/or sounded.

Variation: Blindfold one volunteer. Place an object on the table for him to examine, using all his senses except sight. He then asks questions of the other students to get clues. He cannot ask what it is. Classmates must answer the student's questions truthfully with a *yes, no,* or *sometimes,* but they CAN try to mislead the guesser while still telling the truth. Continue with other "sightless" volunteers and different objects. After the fun, let students examine the objects completely using all their senses. Put away all objects.

Instructions to students: Write a clear description of each object you examined. Describe the object as if you were telling a blind man what it was like. Describe how it looked, felt, sounded, tasted, and smelled.

JOKER   MIXED-UP

Purpose: To stress the importance of putting details in a logical order; to give practice in sequence of thought.

Find four different examples of fiction or nonfiction narratives of the same lengths in old, partially used, or sample workbooks. Cut narratives into parts, and mount each part on tagboard to keep stiff and easy to handle. Put parts on tack board area (out of order) with each narrative separated. Divide the class into four relay teams. (Each team will work on its own narrative.)

Instructions to students: Your team should try to put the narrative in proper sequence as fast as you can. *Each team member* must come to the tack board in order and decide whether or not he wishes to change the sequence. You cannot consult anyone during the game. Read carefully. It may be trickier than you think. The first team to *correctly* sequence the parts, have all team members inspect the sequence, and have their last team member say, "Done!" is the winner.

Variation: Instead of using teams, the cut-up narratives can be put in large envelopes for individual practice in rearranging in a logical sequence. Put numbers on back to show correct order.

INTRO AND FOCUS   SET-UP

Purpose: To provide practice in accurate observation and written recall of events observed; to introduce a problem to be solved and give students an opportunity to offer solutions.

Arrange secretly to have two students burst into the classroom at the beginning of class. Instruct them to have a mock argument, even with a bit of pushing or shoving, and to run out of the room angrily. Students involved in the set-up should then go to the library, agree on exactly what happened, and work out a detailed, written account together. Hand out student worksheet, *EYE WITNESS*.

When the two set-up students return, read the various accounts and different solutions put forth by the observers. Discuss why there is agreement or disagreement on the details, and why these differences may affect the solutions offered. (Students have different vantage points; some are more observant; some tend to exaggerate; people differ in their values, etc.) The final paper read should be the one written by the participants in the set-up.

Variation: Arrange secretly to have THREE students involved in a set-up. Two are working on a project; the third ruins it. This can work naturally when students in the class have been involved in a project for several days and have tangible work to show for their efforts. The project could be a written project, art project or poster, or other endeavor that would appear to take a great deal of time to redo. (It is prudent to substitute a fake project for the real one, so no one really has to begin their project again!)

INTRO   STRING-A-LING SURPRISE

Purpose: To provide an opportunity to create a picture or design to use as the inspiration for a fiction story.

Give each student a piece of string, and make a variety of poster paint colors available.

Instructions to students: Holding tight to one end to keep it clean and dry, dip your string in poster paint. Then swirl and loop the painted string around on a piece of plain paper. Put another sheet of paper on top with the clean part of the string hanging out the bottom. Pull the string out carefully, take off the top sheet, and surprise yourself with your drawing. See *STRING-A-LING STORY*.

Variations: See ABSTRACT ATTRACTIONS, INK BLOTS, SNIP-SNIP, DRIBBLE PIC, RUNAWAY PAINT, LAST STRAW, and ALL THUMBS for ways to concoct artistic designs and pictures to precede story-writing or other creative writing activities. The *STRING-A-LING STORY* reproducible worksheet appropriately follows all these activities.

Focus   *EYE WITNESS*

Name: _____ **Date** _____

Purpose: To provide practice in writing a description of observed events; to figure out a solution to a problem.

Instructions: Write an accurate account of who was involved, what they were wearing, who said what, and anything else you can remember about the incident. Be as detailed and specific as possible. Offer a viable solution to the dilemma.

_____

_____

_____

_____

_____

_____

_____

_____

_____

_____

_____

_____

_____

_____

_____

_____

_____

_____

_____

Focus   ***WHAT SHOULD YOU DO?***

Purpose: To provide experience in writing a solution to a problem or dilemma.

Instructions: Choose one of the following problems or dilemmas. Write two paragraphs. In the first paragraph, state the problem or dilemma and your reactions to the situation; in the second, describe your thoughts on the best solution to the problem.

(1) Your mom tells you that you can't go to the basketball game because you didn't get a good enough grade in English. How do you react? What should you do?

(2) You can't get your locker open, and you're surely going to be late to class. Your teacher is very strict about your being on time. How do you react? What should you do?

(3) Your parents are getting a divorce. You love them both, but they have asked you to choose one of them to live with. How do you react? What should you do?

(4) You find out that a person you thought was your best friend has betrayed your confidence. She told others secrets that you told her never to tell. How do you react? What should you do?

(5) Your boyfriend (or girlfriend) does not want to hang around with you anymore. How do you react? What should you do?

(6) Your teacher thinks you have cheated on a test. (You haven't.) How do you react? What should you do?

(7) Your teacher thinks you have cheated on a test. (You have.) How do you react? What should you do?

(8) Your parents have grounded you for breaking one of their rules. How do you react? What should you do?

(9) There is a bully who keeps picking on you when no one is looking. How do you react? What do you do?

(10) You know you are going to get a failing grade in one class. Your parents don't have the slightest idea that you have not been doing well. How do you react? What do you do?

(11) Students are making fun of you for some reason (the way you dress, the way you wear your hair, your big nose, your inability in gym, or other reason). How do you react? What do you do?

MONSTER MADNESS

Purpose: To stimulate imagination; to create a unique character and use it in an original story; to show uniqueness of each individual character.

Instructions: Make your name about 2 inches high and 5 inches from beginning to end. Then repeat the same letters the same size directly on top of your first ones.

Now turn your paper a quarter turn to the right. To make your name look like a monster, draw an enclosure (oval, round, square, or whatever) around the whole thing to represent the face. Add hair, hat, or something else to make it look like a monster.

Write a short story about your monster. Name him, her, or it, and have him get into (or cause someone else to get into) three problems. Then solve the problems with a believable and interesting ending.

Staple the monster picture you have created onto the top of your story. Don't put your name on your story. We should be able to guess whose monster it is by deciphering the name and last initial used to create your monster.

INTRO   **ABSTRACT ATTRACTIONS**

Purpose: To provide an opportunity to create a picture or design to use as inspiration for a fictional story.

Instructions to students: Take your pencil and make a series of large, overlapping and looping curves (squiggles). Fill in areas with solid colors, dots, stripes, or other designs. See *STRING-A-LING STORY*.

INTRO   **INK BLOTS**

Purpose: To provide an opportunity to create a picture or design to use as the basis for a fiction story.

Use an eye-dropper to put ink blots on the papers of students. Older, well-coordinated students can probably drop their own ink blobs onto their papers.
Instructions to students: I will place three ink blots on your piece of paper. Then fold the paper in half either lengthwise or sideways. Wait a few moments for it to dry. Open the paper up and see what you created! See *STRING-A-LING STORY* to follow up.

INTRO   **SNIP-SNIP**

Purpose: To provide an opportunity to create a picture or design to use as a foundation for a fiction story.

Distribute paper and scissors to each student.
Instructions to students: Fold your paper in half, and cut out a few snips. Do not unfold it, but fold again the other way, and cut out a few more snips. Continue this twice more so you have folded your paper a total of four times. Now open it up and see what it reminds you of. Follow up with *STRING-A-LING STORY*.

INTRO   **DRIBBLE PIC**

Purpose: To provide an opportunity to create a picture or design to use as a spark for fictional story-writing.

Distribute white glue (not paste or transparent glue) and colored construction paper.
Instructions to students: Dribble the glue around on the paper, making an interesting picture. What does it remind you of? Follow up with *STRING-A-LING STORY*.

INTRO   **RUNAWAY PAINT**

Purpose: To provide an opportunity to create a picture or design to use as a stimulus for a fiction story.

Provide poster paint or control the paint yourself (less messy). Drop three or four drops of paint on each student's paper. If you use more than one color (or different colors for various students), it develops more distinctive designs and pictures.

Instructions to students: I'm going to drop three or four drops of poster paint on your paper. Have your papers ready for me as I come around to your desk. As soon as I put the droplets on your paper, hold it up to let the paint run across the paper. BEFORE IT RUNS OFF THE EDGE, change directions. Keep changing directions until the paint stops running. Blow gently on it or flop the paper in the air *carefully* to make it dry quickly. What does it remind you of?

Hints: A blow-dryer (for hair) speeds up the drying process, and old grocery sacks work well for the paper. Follow this activity with story-writing. See *STRING-A-LING STORY*.

INTRO   **LAST STRAW**

Purpose: To provide an opportunity to create a picture or design to use as an impetus for a fictional story.

You will need poster paint, paper, and drinking straws. Cut the straws in half if you need to economize. Drop three or four blobs of paint onto the paper of each student.

Instructions to students: Blow through your straw to distribute the paint into a design or picture. Move the straw to any blob area until the paint is spread out. Continue until no more blobs are evident. What does it remind you of? Follow up with *STRING-A-LING STORY*.

INTRO   **ALL THUMBS**

Purpose: To create a picture or design to use as an idea for a fictional story; to show the uniqueness of each individual.

Have students make a personal thumbprint (or several overlapping prints) with the help of an ink pad and paper. Point out how each person has distinctly different lines and whorls which show his uniqueness. Have students color parts of the designs, and decide what they look like. Continue with *STRING-A-LING STORY*.

Focus   *STRING-A-LING STORY*

Name _____ Date _____

Purpose: To write a fictional narrative using a picture or design you have uniquely created.

Instructions: Think about your picture or design. Turn it sideways, upside down, or partway around.

What does it remind you of?_____

What does it make you think about?_____

_____

Does it look like a person, a monster, an animal, a tree, or what? _____

Write a short, fictional narrative about anything your picture or design suggests to you.

_____

_____

_____

_____

_____

_____

_____

_____

_____

_____

_____

_____

_____

_____

INTRO AND FOCUS   **CLAY CHARACTER**

Purpose: To form a character (person or animal) from modeling clay to use as inspiration for a character in an original story.

Provide enough modeling clay for each student to create a character for a story. Ten minutes' modeling should produce satisfactory results.

Instructions to students: Use the character you have created as a major character in an original story, and name him or her if you wish. Tell at least three adventures your character has, and end the story with a surprise ending.

JOKER   **CLASS BOOK**

Purpose: To provide an interesting and constructive free-time activity for students whose work is completed; to build self-esteem.

Put a collection of diversified writings of classmates into an appropriately labeled folder for student reading during their free time. (They love it!)

Variation: Put the collection together with paper fasteners and ask a student volunteer to design and make an original cover for it.

INTRO   **ANIMALISMS**

Purpose: To provide a personal, unique shape to represent an animal character for use in a creative, fictional story.

Give each student a strip of paper (about one-third of a lengthwise division of construction paper). If you don't have time to pre-cut them, the better students can fold the paper into thirds lengthwise and tear the strips carefully so each student has one strip. You can even have students fold their own lined writing paper, but plain white or construction paper works best.

Each student folds his strip in half and prints his name along the edge of the fold. Be sure he uses a capital letter at the beginning of his name and small letters for the rest. This assures a bumpy shape. He then sketches a line closely around the shape of the letters and cuts around the line. (He must not cut along the fold itself.)

When he opens up the folded sheet, he will find an unusual shape. He then turns it over, adds eyes, ears, hair, or whatever he wishes to complete his unique animal.

The *ANIMALISMS* worksheet gives complete instructions for students to make their animals, and specific directions for their writing assignment.

Variation: Animals made from names with little variation in letter shapes are rather plain. (For example, Jane does not produce a very interesting shape.) If this happens, suggest using the month of the student's birthday instead of his name. Again, be certain the first letter of the month is capitalized to form a more appealing shape.

Focus   *ANIMALISMS*

Name _____   Date _____

    Purpose: To create a unique animal character and use it as the main character in an original story.

    Instructions: Place your paper strip on your desk so it is longest from top to bottom. Fold your paper in half with the bottom coming up toward the top. (The fold will be at the bottom.)

    Print your first name only, beginning *as close as possible* to the folded edge (bottom). Be sure to use a capital letter at the beginning of your name and small letters thereafter.

    Then outline the name by drawing a pencil line closely around the shape of your letters. DO NOT DRAW ANY LINES ON THE FOLD. Cut out this shape before you unfold your paper. Now add appendages (arms, legs, eyes, whiskers, or whatever is needed) on the back to make a real or make-believe animal.

    Use the animal you have created as a major character in an original story, and name him or her if you wish. Tell at least three adventures your character has, and end the story with a surprise ending. You will need to use both sides of this sheet.

_____

_____

_____

_____

_____

_____

_____

_____

_____

_____

_____

_____

_____

_____

INTRO   **TELL A TALL ONE**

Purpose: To trick the students into almost believing a tall tale you are telling or reading to them; to introduce students to tall tales and legends before they write one of their own.

Tell a modern tall tale. Fool them into partially believing you by beginning the tale fairly logically and pretending you are recounting an experience that happened to someone you know. (If you use the name of one of the other teachers in your building, it is even more fun!) Then exaggerate more and more. Try to tell the tale as seriously as you can, acting as if you really believe it, even though it could not possibly be true with its gross exaggeration.

If you can think up your own tall tale, you can personalize it to your hometown situation. If not, use *A CAT'S TALE* and substitute someone the students know for Mrs. McGregor's name.

INTRO   **SHORT AND SWEET**

Purpose: To introduce the concept of a topic sentence by analyzing a picture.

Show a picture. Elicit the shortest possible sentence about it that expresses the main idea. Write it on the board, and discuss how this could be the topic sentence for a composition. Add words as needed to add meaning and clarity.

Show a second picture. Again, work it through together in the same way, deciding on a brief sentence, then elaborating on it.

Then show a third picture. Each student should decide on the main idea and write the topic sentence for this picture by himself. Continue with SHORT AND SWEET PARAGRAPHS.

Do any of you know Mrs McGregor's mother? She is old and doesn't see very well anymore. She had a cat named Poco. She said she called him Poco because Poco meant "Little One" in Spanish. Anyway, he was so tiny he fit into the chair with her and was hardly noticed. Poco was little, would cuddle into her lap easily, and was a great companion.

In her effort to take excellent care of her cat, Mrs. McGregor's mother decided to give him a special, powdered cat food supplement. It was supposed to make him healthy and have a glossy coat because it was loaded with vitamins and minerals.

She started sprinkling the powder over his food at suppertime as the box directed, and indeed, he *did* start to grow. Before she knew it, he could no longer sit in the comfortable chair with her; in fact, he couldn't even fit into the chair by himself! Poco kept getting larger . . . and LARGER . . . and *LARGER.*

Soon he was having trouble squeezing through the door. Then he became the talk of the neighborhood. He kept on growing until he was so huge people decided to make special uses of his strength and size.

Poco liked being useful. He didn't mind yowling as a warning siren for the whole community in time of fire or emergency. He put up with the church bell around his neck and rang it for them every Sunday. He didn't complain when he had to plow furrows with his giant claws so the farmers could plant their corn. He even enjoyed digging to help them reroute lakes and rivers. But Poco *did* kind of resent having to walk around all the time with his tail straight up, just so the red, blinking light tied to his tail could warn low-flying airplanes!

Everyone wondered and wondered why Poco was so monstrously large. Finally they discovered Mrs. McGregor was sprinkling his powder out of the wrong jar. Her old eyes just weren't what they once had been, and she was giving him SUPER PLANT FOOD instead of SUPPER CAT FOOD! She, of course, stopped this at once, and slowly, almost imperceptibly, he began shrinking.

The big yowl became fainter and fainter, and he could no longer be the siren; the bell grew too heavy and slipped off his smaller neck; his claws were too small to help the farmers with their planting, and his paws too weak to dig waterways. And when they finally took the blinking light off his tail, he purred and purred and purred his appreciation!

Mrs. McGregor's mother knew he was back to normal when she sat down in her comfortable chair and there was Poco, almost unnoticed in the corner. Sure, it has made him feel important to be big and useful, but Poco was glad to be the lovable, "Little One" again!

Do you believe this story? Of course, it isn't true; it's a tall tale, like the one about Paul Bunyan and his ox, Babe. They're fun to hear and think about, aren't they? They're even more fun to make up. Today you're going to write your own tall tale, and you can have fun by exaggerating as much as you like.

FOCUS   **SHORT AND SWEET PARAGRAPHS**

Purpose: To develop a paragraph from a topic sentence formulated from the main idea of a picture. For introduction, see SHORT AND SWEET.

Instructions to students: Write one paragraph beginning with the topic sentence you decide upon. Stick to the topic by giving details relating to this main idea. We will have some of you read your paragraphs to the class, and tell why you chose your particular topic sentences. There are many "right" ways to write this paragraph.

JOKER   **VERY TOPICAL**

Purpose: To provide review and practice in finding topic sentences in paragraphs; to reconstruct a paragraph based on its main idea.

Bring and encourage students to bring many newspapers to the classroom. Distribute at least 1 news page to each student.

Instructions to students: Choose one paragraph from the newspaper, and write down the two or three most important words in its topic sentence. Trade your paper with a friend, and using his main idea words, write a short paragraph reconstructing the meaning of his paragraph without looking at the original article.

After students have completed their reconstructions of paragraphs, take turns reading aloud the original paragraphs, the words chosen from the topic sentence to summarize the main idea, and the reconstructed paragraphs. Discuss problems rewriting the paragraph (poor choices of main words or inability to recognize topic sentences) and the value of recognizing topic sentences.

Variation: Substitute magazines for newspapers.

INTRO   **STRETCH LIMOUSINE**

Purpose: To introduce wordiness; to emphasize the undesirability of using unnecessary words.

Before students enter, write an exceptionally long and overly involved sentence on the chalkboard. Write as much of the sentence as possible horizontally to emphasize length. (Use several chalkboards wide, rather than continuing too much of the sentence underneath.) By sketching an outline around it, you can make the sentence look very much like a long, stretch limousine!

Working together, trim the sentence to suitable length. Call on students to come to the board to institute changes. When they finish, draw an outline around the new, more efficient compact car.

Wordy example:

As the big fiery orange,
blazing, beautiful sun disappeared
slowly, quietly, and ever so beautifully into
the glistening, sparkling, blue, deep waters of the churning, bubbling, wavy ocean,
Jerry, clad in ragged, tight, torn blue jeans sat thoughtfully, pensively, and in silence on the sandy and grassy green, sloping shoreline, thinking of his handsome,
good-looking, older brother, Jim, who had recently married the dull dodo, Dora.

Improved example:

As the fiery orange sun quietly

disappeared into the glistening, deep waves

of the ocean, Jerry, in his ragged jeans sat pensively

on the sandy shoreline, thinking of his handsome, older brother,

Jim, who had recently married a very unintelligent girl named Dora.

Variation: Run copies of a wordy short story. Have students make the deletions on their own copies. See *STRETCH LIMOUSINE*.

Focus *STRETCH LIMOUSINE*

Name _____ Date _____

Purpose: To emphasize the undesirability of being too wordy.

Instructions to students: This story is much too wordy! Make the stretch limousine into a more compact and efficient vehicle by deleting unnecessary words. Make the corrections on this sheet, trying to fill in only the lines shown below the story. Draw an outline of the car and a couple of wheels to complete the picture.

"Stop. Stop, I say. Stop! Stop! Stop! Stop! Stop!" the wrinkled, bearded, old man in a tattered, grey, double-breasted, wool suit shouted loudly and boisterously, as loudly as he could possibly shout.

I, resting quietly and alone in my soft, comfortable, king-size bed in my green, yellow, and white, Colonial-style bedroom, wondered quizzically what was happening. I sprang rapidly, but carefully to my feet, which were aching from my exercises the previous, sunny, but glorious day, and opened wide the window on the north side of my home, which was dirty and streaked from a violent wind and dust storm the previous day. I saw through my sleepy, blue eyes the shadowly form of the old man in his grey, tattered, double-breasted, wool suit.

"What is the problem you are having, if I may ask without being too overly rude?" I asked tentatively and hestitatingly. Then I finally noticed what all the shouting and carrying on was all about. A tiny, little, mousy-grey mouse had mischievously, but surprisingly, darted up his wide, grey, pinstriped pant leg!

_____

_____

_____

_____

_____

_____

_____

Section II

READING AND LITERATURE

INTRO **ANALYZING ADS**

Purpose: To introduce an assignment on advertising; to analyze ads to see how they consciously appeal to people's needs; to encourage discernment and judgment in evaluating advertisements.

Pass out magazines, at least one to each student. They need not be current. Ask each student to cut out three advertisements. Do not tell students what they will be doing with the ads, or students may choose only ads they feel are easy to analyze.

When they have finished, ask them to look at their own ads and determine how each ad appeals to people. As they bring out different appeals, put the major categories on the chalkboard. You will probably have examples of ads appealing to the following needs: enjoyment, love, sex, security, patriotism, hero worship, greed (to possess things), self-image, adventure, to be part of an "in" group, creativity, and having a long, healthful life.

Discuss specific appeals to needs, and have students vote on the most effective ads. Follow up with an attractive bulletin board, showing the most compelling ads grouped by categories of needs met.

INTRO **ADVANCE PUBLICITY**

Purpose: To "advertise" upcoming events (literary selections or stories students will be reading); to spark interest and curiosity about the next classwork.

Use your bulletin board as a billboard. Put pictures on it relating to forthcoming stories, but omit names of stories or authors. Include little-known facts or especially interesting or unusual tidbits about the author or story. Following are examples of author facts that might pique student interest; others could focus on the literary work or story. Example:

DO YOU KNOW THIS JACK?

Son of Pioneers

Newsboy

Gang Member

Called Himself a Drunken Bum

(Interest-getter for Jack London before reading *Call of the Wild.*)

Example:

> STEPHEN WHO?
>
> Born in a Parsonage (Father a Minister)
>
> 14th Child in Family
>
> Almost Died in Shipwreck at Sea
>
> Died at Early Age of 29

(Develop curiosity for Stephen Crane's *The Red Badge of Courage*.)

Example:

> GUESS WHO?
>
> Orphaned at Age Two; Adopted
>
> Ran Away to Join Army
>
> Dismissed from West Point

(Introduce students to Edgar Allan Poe and his work.)

INTRO   GOOD MORNING

Purpose: To advertise for several days in advance of reading a story involving foreign phrases; to invoke attention.

Start class every day for a few days prior to reading a story containing foreign words or phrases by saying "Good Morning" or "Good-bye" in another language. Examples: bonjour (French); guten Morgen (German); buenos dias (Spanish); au revoir (French); auf Wiedershen (German); adios (Spanish). If you are fluent in a foreign language, you can take this attention-getting even further.

TANTALIZING ADS

Purpose: To entice others to read a book or story.

Instructions: Choose one of the following ways to advertise your book or story:

1. Tape-record or videotape an advertisement.

2. Design an enticing book cover.

3. Make a bulletin board or mural advertisement.

4. Make a collage advertisement from magazine pictures.

5. Deliver an oral advertisement, as a television announcer or carnival barker might.

6. Create a poster advertisement.

7. Create a brochure advertisement.

8. Illustrate specific scenes and put a caption on each.

9. Make a hanging mobile advertisement (use characters or objects important to the story).

10. Use the computer to create and print out an advertisement.

For numbers 1 and 5, choose a story that is suspenseful, humorous, or descriptive. Choose a part (two to three minutes long) that is particularly interesting, and copy it on note-cards. Don't tell the climax or ending. Tell title, author, and read excerpt with feeling, trying to get others in the class to read the story.

Caution: Do not try to tell the whole plot. You are advertising the book or story and trying to get others to read it, not giving a book report or summary.

JOKER   **DO YOU SEE WHAT I SEE?**

Purpose: To practice sound discrimination and alliteration.

Put the word *alliteration* on the chalkboard in large letters.
You: I see something in the classroom beginning with the "c" sound. (If you are thinking of the calendar, use an alliterative adjective to describe it.) It is a *classy* what? If you see what I see, raise your hand and guess. Take all guesses offered. If a student guesses any item with the same sound (not necessarily spelled with the same first letter), he is correct. If he is incorrect, explain why.
Continue: I see something in the classroom beginning with the "b" sound. It is a *big* what? (Perhaps it is a bookcase.) Again, hear all guesses one at a time.
Frequently repeat the terms, *alliteration* and *alliterative,* to firmly establish them in students' minds. After a correct response, say: "Yes, that is an example of alliteration. The same beginning sound is repeated." Students can take turns being the leader in this game after they understand how to play it.

INTRO   **TONGUE-TWISTERS**

Purpose: To introduce a lesson on alliteration.

Have a series of tongue-twisters written on the chalkboard for students to view as they come in. (They will immediately begin to practice them!) Let them choose one to perfect. Give them five minutes to practice saying it three times in a row as quickly as they can. This gets a bit noisy, but is all in good fun.
Have students recite twisters to the class as fast as they can. The more mistakes they make, the more they seem to enjoy it. Be prepared, because they will challenge you to try it, too.
Some tricky old standbys:

> Better buy a bigger rubber baby buggy bumper.
> Silly Sally's sewing shirts for soldiers.
> Peter Piper picked a peck of pickled peppers.

A few new ones:

> Gordie the goalie got a great goal.
> Tardy Tillie tapped her terrible toes tentatively.
> Laughing Lena laid her lawn chair along the lake side.

After the fun ask why tongue-twisters are so difficult to say. (They will tell you there are too many sounds alike at the beginnings of the words.) Discuss use of sound repetitions to create certain effects.

Name_____ Date _____

Purpose: To firmly instill the concept and terminology of alliteration by overusing and having fun with it.

Instructions: Read the examples about Cary, the cat-carver, and Mary's moon-faced marionette. Then make up a short, silly story of your own, using as much alliteration as you can, and write it on the lines below the examples.

You may use a dictionary to give you ideas and spellings. *Circle all alliteration.* When everyone is finished, we will have fun reading the alliterative paragraphs aloud. Examples:

Cary, the crackpot cat-carver, created candlesticks, canaries, cards, and cans. He cut out candy canes, canoes, and calendars. What else do you think Cary craved to carve?

Mary, the millionaire, made a moon-faced marionette. Men from Mercury and Mars merged on her mansion and manhandled the mannequin. The Martian mayor and mighty military men met with Mary and said the mayhem was misunderstood. Their men had mistaken the marionette for magic and had been mystified by her mercurial movements.

_____

_____

_____

_____

_____

_____

_____

_____

_____

_____

_____

_____

INTRO   **BIO/AUTOBIO**

Purpose: To contrast biography and autobiography.

Present derivation of the two words to help students remember the terminology. Examples:
Biography comes from the Greek words
bios = life   graphos = writing
Thus a biography is the writing of someone's life story.
Autobiography comes from the Greek words
autos = self   bios = life   graphos = writing
Thus an autobiography is the story of someone's life written by himself.
Variation: You can elicit meanings of *bio, graph,* and *auto* from older or sharper students by putting derived words on the chalkboard. Examples: biology, biopsy, bionic; telegraph, graphics, graphology; automobile, automatic, autograph. They then can deduce the difference between biography and autobiography.

JOKER   **BOOK FAIR**

Purpose: To encourage reading and book-buying; to open students' minds to the wealth of wholesome, exciting reading material available; to raise money.

Putting on a book fair takes advanced planning; it's time-consuming and energy-taxing. (You have been warned!) The results, however, far outweigh the effort expended. If you can spur your librarian to put it on, great! If you can't, you can cut down on the work by having a book distributor pick out and deliver all books and materials to the school. You will still have to arrange for getting the display set up and torn down, time and place for showing, and people to help.

Students, parents, administrators, and other teachers react positively to this project. A two-day time frame (including one evening for parents) is ample. Use of the library or gym is usually required to accommodate the display and sale. The school gets a percentage of profits, and the money can be used to finance other projects for your language arts program.

FOCUS   **NOVEL AND STORY REPORTS**

Purpose: To check up on fiction reading; to reinforce the structure of fiction.

It is important to check up on outside reading and to give credit and encouragement for student efforts outside of class. Use the *NOVEL REPORT* for more sophisticated readers, the *STORY REPORT* for less experienced students. *WHAT I THINK ABOUT MY STORY* gives younger children an opportunity to evaluate a story and express their opinions while allowing the teacher to see if the student understood the main points.
These report forms help students conceptualize the main parts of fiction writing without being so detailed and cumbersome as to deter reading. Their brevity avoids burdensome teacher evaluation. They provide you with opportunities to evaluate understandings of student reading and thereby to guide their future reading.

Focus

NOVEL REPORT

Name_____ Date_____

NAME OF BOOK _____

AUTHOR_____ NUMBER OF PAGES_____

SETTING (Time and Place) _____

MAIN CHARACTERS (Name and briefly describe each.)

_____

_____

_____

CONFLICT (Problem) _____

_____

PLOT (List main incidents in order.)

_____

_____

_____

_____

_____

SUBPLOTS, IF ANY (List less important threads of story.)

_____

_____

RESOLUTION OF CONFLICT (How was problem resolved?)

_____

YOUR REACTIONS (Did it hold your interest? Why or why not?)

_____

_____

Focus   *STORY REPORT*

Name_____ Date_____

NAME OF STORY _____

AUTHOR _____

SETTING _____

    WHEN _____

    WHERE _____

CHARACTERS AND SOMETHING ABOUT EACH

_____

_____

_____

_____

PROBLEM

_____

_____

_____

EVENTS (IN ORDER THAT THEY HAPPENED)

_____

_____

_____

_____

_____

SOLUTION TO PROBLEM

_____

_____

TOTAL PAGES IN STORY_____ DID YOU LIKE IT?_____

Focus   ***WHAT I THINK ABOUT MY STORY***

Name_____ Date_____

TITLE OF STORY _____

1. WHO OR WHAT IS THE STORY MAINLY ABOUT?

_____

2. TELL WHAT HE, SHE, OR IT IS LIKE.

_____

3. WHERE DOES THE STORY TAKE PLACE?

_____

4. WHEN DOES THE STORY TAKE PLACE?

_____

5. IN WHAT WAY DOES SOMETHING IN THE STORY REMIND YOU OF *YOU* (EITHER A PERSON OR SOMETHING THAT HAPPENED)?

_____

6. WHAT IN THE STORY MAKES YOU HAPPY OR SAD?

_____

7. IF YOU COULD CHANGE SOMETHING ABOUT THE STORY, EXPLAIN WHAT YOU WOULD CHANGE AND HOW YOU WOULD CHANGE IT.

_____

_____

8. WHICH STATEMENTS TELL YOUR FEELINGS ABOUT THE STORY?
____ THIS WAS A GREAT STORY.
____ MY FRIENDS SHOULD READ THIS STORY.
____ THIS WAS AN O.K. STORY.
____ I DIDN'T UNDERSTAND THIS STORY.
____ MY FRIENDS WOULD NOT LIKE THIS STORY.

Focus   *ALTERNATIVE BOOK REPORTS*

Purpose: To give you more choice and to encourage your creativity.

Instructions: You may choose one of the following instead of a regular book report.

1. Summarize the book or story.

2. Do a one-page analysis and description of one of the characters in the book or story.

3. Write one page of short descriptions of the main characters in the book or story. Use *DESCRIPTIONS*.

4. Write a one-page report on the author of the book or story. See *AUTHOR RE-PORT*.

5. Create an original fifteen-clue crossword puzzle using clues and answers from the book or story. Use *CROSSWORD*.

6. Choose one or more quotations from the book or story and explain why they have special meaning for you. Use *QUOTES*.

7. Create five original sketches of scenes, characters, or other items which relate to the book or story.

8. Write a different ending for the book or story.

9. Write a one-page essay using one of the topic sentences below. Use *ESSAY*.

   a. This book should be read by anyone who doesn't like to read.

   b. I felt like this book was written about me.

   c. This book should be buried in a time capsule so it could be re-trieved in the year 2090.

   d. This book helped me understand myself better.

10. Compare and contrast yourself to one of the characters in the book or story. Use *COMPARE/CONTRAST*.

11. Find ten new words you learned from the book or story. List them, define them IN YOUR OWN WORDS, and give one example of how to use each word. Use *NEW VOCAB-ULARY*.

12. Write a friendly letter (in correct format with addressed envelope) to the author or to a character in your book or story.

13. Prepare an oral report using a flannel board to emphasize major and minor points. Use an outline or web to organize your thoughts.

DESCRIPTIONS

Name_____ Date_____

Instructions: Describe each of the main characters in the book or story you have read. Be detailed, and show the relationships existing among them.

Protagonist _____

_____

_____

_____

_____

Antagonist _____

_____

_____

_____

_____

Other _____

_____

_____

_____

_____

_____

_____

Other _____

_____

_____

_____

_____

Focus   ***AUTHOR REPORT***

Name_____ **Date**_____

Instructions: Write a report on the author of the book or story you have read. You can use the back of this sheet to finish if needed. Name the author; describe his early life; tell about his education and early adulthood; report on his family relationships; describe any unusual things about him or his writing.

CROSSWORD

Instructions: Make up an original 15-clue crossword puzzle using clues and answers from the book or story you have read. Put your puzzle on this side and your answers on the back of this paper.

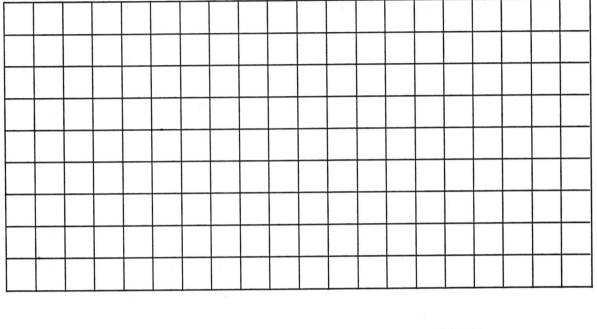

ACROSS

_____

_____

_____

_____

_____

_____

_____

_____

_____

_____

DOWN

_____

_____

_____

_____

_____

_____

_____

_____

_____

_____

Focus   ***QUOTES***

Name_____ **Date**_____

Instructions: Choose two quotations from the book or story you have read. Write the quotations, and explain why they have special meaning for you.

Quotation: _____

_____

_____

_____

_____

Why It Is Meaningful to ME _____

_____

_____

_____

_____

_____

Quotation: _____

_____

_____

_____

Why It Is Meaningful to ME _____

_____

_____

_____

_____

Focus   ***ESSAY***

Name_____ **Date**_____

Instructions: Use your own paper to write a one-page essay using one of the following topic sentences:

1. This book should be read by anyone who doesn't like to read.

2. I felt like this book was written about me.

3. This book should be buried in a time capsule so it could be retrieved in the year 2090.

4. This book helped me understand myself better.

Fill out the answers to the questions below, and staple this paper on top of your essay. Hand the two pages in together.

NAME OF BOOK?_____

AUTHOR _____

TOPIC SENTENCE? _____1 _____2 _____3 _____4

Focus   ***COMPARE/ CONTRAST***

Name_____ Date_____

Instructions: Write two detailed paragraphs. In the first paragraph, compare yourself to one of the characters in the book or story. In the second paragraph, contrast yourself with either the same or a different character.

I am like _____ in many ways. _____

_____

_____

_____

_____

_____

_____

_____

_____

_____

I am not like _____ in many ways._____

_____

_____

_____

_____

_____

_____

_____

_____

Focus   ***NEW VOCABULARY***

Name _____ Date_____

Instructions: Find seven new words you learned from the book or story. List them, and define them *in your own words*. Give an example of how to use each word.

1. WORD _____

   DEFINITION _____

   EXAMPLE OF USE _____

2. WORD _____

   DEFINITION _____

   EXAMPLE OF USE _____

3. WORD _____

   DEFINITION _____

   EXAMPLE OF USE _____

4. WORD _____

   DEFINITION _____

   EXAMPLE OF USE _____

5. WORD _____

   DEFINITION _____

   EXAMPLE OF USE _____

6. WORD _____

   DEFINITION _____

   EXAMPLE OF USE _____

7. WORD _____

   DEFINITION _____

   EXAMPLE OF USE _____

Focus   *GUILTY OR INNOCENT?*

Name_____ Date_____

    Purpose: To analyze a character from a story you have read; to decide whether the hero is totally good or if the villain is totally bad.

    Instructions: We will choose a prosecutor, defense attorney, and judge. The rest of the class will be the jury. As the trial proceeds, jot down points for and against the character. Base your thoughts on solid evidence.

CHARACTER _____ HERO OR VILLAIN? _____

POINTS FOR CHARACTER   POINTS AGAINST CHARACTER

_____   _____

_____   _____

_____   _____

_____   _____

_____   _____

_____   _____

_____   _____

_____   _____

_____   _____

YOUR DECISION: IS THE CHARACTER TOTALLY GOOD OR TOTALLY EVIL? EXPLAIN YOUR DECISION.

_____

_____

_____

_____

_____

_____

MAKE THE SCENE

Purpose: To dramatize scenes from reading selections; to enjoy pretending to be the characters; to learn to improvise.

Instructions: An improvisation is an extemporaneous spur-of-the-moment project. You will perform with only a small amount of advance planning and will have to make up your dialogue and actions as you go along.

1. Divide into groups containing three or four students.

2. Choose a story you have studied recently that would be fun to act out.

3. Divide the story into a series of three scenes.

4. Decide as a group the following:

   a. What character will each student play?
   b. Where do the scenes take place?
   c. How does each scene begin?
   d. How does each scene end?
   e. What costumes or props do you have readily available?

5. You will be given ten minutes for planning.

6. Your group's total improvisation presentation is limited to ten minutes, so individual scenes should run two or three minutes.

7. Each group will perform their scenes for the rest of the class. The audience will try to identify the story.

REMEMBER: The dialogue and exact happenings should be improvised, rather than written down, though your group should discuss the general plan ahead of time. Use the space below or the back of this sheet to jot down your plan.

JOKER   **WHO AM I?**

Purpose: To emphasize characterization; to have fun with characters.

Give one student a slip of paper with the name of a character from a story the class has read within the last month. Tell the student to pretend he is that character, to act like him, speak like him, and answer questions as he would.

Other students ask questions to try to guess who he is. He must answer truthfully. When that character is guessed correctly, the one who guesses it becomes a new character.

After students get used to this game, they can be the character they choose, and you won't have to give them the slips of paper. (They prefer to choose their own characters.)

Variation: Pick typical dialogue from the story. Read it. Ask "Who am I?" If students cannot guess, you can read other bits of dialogue for further clues.

Variation: Ask students to choose typical dialogue from the story, read it, and ask, "Who am I?" If classmates cannot guess, the reader can choose other examples to provide help. The student who guesses the character correctly then reads his selected dialogue. The game continues in this manner.

INTRO   **LISTEN FOR CLUES**

Purpose: To introduce the idea of context clues; to let students know that if they read or listen carefully, they can guess meanings of words or happenings by the words leading up to and surrounding the items they do not know; to develop reading comprehension.

Read a short story to them orally. Stop at certain parts to let them guess what words come next or to ask meanings of unfamiliar words. Also stop at intervals to see if they can guess what happens next. The object here is not to trick them, but to allow success in picking up context clues.

You can use the following sentences to give students practice in finding clues before you read a whole story. Slashes show possible places for strategic pauses.

1. The *seismograph* showed the earthquake's force//to be extremely strong.
2. Nocturnal animals like to be awake at night//and sleep during the day.
3. His testimony in court was so *credible* that every juror believed//his story.
4. Since he was just a *novice* at skiing, he had to take lessons from an expert.
5. When the storm *abated,* the sun shone//brightly in the classroom windows.
6. The *genial* student talked, laughed, and otherwise cheered up//her classmates.
7. The junior high dictionary was *abridged* and therefore too small//to include the word I wanted to find.
8. The teacher's help was *indispensable;*// without it, John could never have passed the course.
9. The *velocity* of the baseball was over ninety miles per hour.

Focus

SAME OR DIFFERENT

Name_____ Date_____

Purpose: To develop critical reading and comprehension skills.

Instructions: Put *S* or *D* in front of each pair of statements. If the statements mean exactly the same, put *S;* if the statements mean different things, put *D.*

___ 1. Canada is north of the United States.
    The United States is south of Canada.

___ 2. September is the month after August.
    August is the month before September.

___ 3. The brother of John and Mary is tall.
    John and Mary are shorter than their brother.

___ 4. Texas is south of southern Colorado.
    Colorado is north of northern Texas.

___ 5. Six plus two equals three plus five.
    Six times two equals three times five.

___ 6. The sister of Carla and Marie is the shortest.
    Carla and Marie are shorter than their sister.

___ 7. Each of the five girls had a quarter.
    The girls had five quarters each.

___ 8. The boys had three cousins each.
    Each of the three boys were cousins.

___ 9. *X* comes before *Y* in the alphabet.
    Y comes after *X* in the alphabet.

___10. Friday comes after Thursday.
    Thursday comes after Wednesday.

___11. Marlo was divorced three times.
    Marlo has three husbands.

___12. Tom has five sisters.
    Five girls have a brother, Tom.

WHAT IS OUT OF PLACE?

Purpose: To enhance critical reading skills; to develop categorizing skills.

Instructions: Circle the word that is out of place in each of the following groups.

1. nail	hammer	screw driver	wrench
2. Monday	Thursday	Saturday	November
3. man	woman	boy	male
4. fingers	nose	mouth	eyes
5. ring	finger	necklace	earrings
6. cat	dog	hamster	elephant
7. knife	glass	fork	spoon
8. book	pen	pencil	felt pen
9. computer	calculator	typewriter	movie
10. father	mother	cousin	brother
11. pear	banana	strawberries	celery
12. Ben	Tom	Jane	Dick

Focus   *FAIRY TALE MAP*

Name_____ Date_____

Purpose: To invoke an understanding of aspects common to most fairy tales; to check on comprehension of outside reading.

Instructions: Fill out the Fairy Tale Map completely.

Name of Fairy Tale: _____

Author: _____

Heroine or Hero (Good): _____

Villain (Evil): _____

Opening Phrase or Sentence: _____

_____

Realistic Incidents: _____

_____

_____

_____

Fantasy Incidents: _____

_____

_____

_____

Magic Used: _____

_____

_____

Ending Phrase or Sentence: _____

_____

INTRO   **FICTION VERSUS NONFICTION**

Purpose: To help students remember the terminology and difference between fiction and nonfiction.

This is a real problem for most students. They MISTAKENLY relate the *non* part of nonfiction to *not* true, and get off on the wrong track.

Always explain fiction first. Tell them *fiction* is a *figment* of the imagination—a *flight* of *fancy.* Give examples of fiction writing. Be sure they fully understand what fiction means before continuing.

Then move to the explanation of nonfiction. Nonfiction is *not* fiction. Thus it is real. Give examples.

FOCUS   **FACT AND FICTION**

Purpose: To learn to differentiate between fact and fiction.

After students research a topic, have them write fictional stories based on facts and read them to the class. Discuss the differences between the factual and fictional portions of the accounts.

Variation: After researching a topic, have students write one page of fact and one page of fiction on the same topic. Put the pages together in a class booklet. Be sure each page is labeled with the topic and marked fact or fiction or arranged with all fiction together and all nonfiction together.

JOKER   **CAN YOU FOLLOW DIRECTIONS?**

Purpose: To have fun while giving practice in reading and following directions.

This exercise involves giving students written directions. Students divide their papers into six approximately equal sections, and respond using their pencils and papers. The first person done can be rewarded with a privilege.

On the next pages are three reproducible worksheets dealing with following written directions. The first two require pencil-and-paper responses; the last one requires physical responses.

FOLLOWING DIRECTIONS (Easy Paper/Pencil Version) is designed for younger students; *FOLLOWING DIRECTIONS* (Difficult Paper/Pencil Version) is for more advanced students. The last worksheet, *FOLLOWING DIRECTIONS* (Physical Directions Version) is mostly for fun and suitable for all ages. In all cases you should give *no* help whatsoever. Remember the purpose—to see if students can follow directions by themselves!

Variation: For younger or slower students, have them divide papers into *four* sections, and give simpler directions.

Variation: You can *read* the directions to students (without distributing copies of the worksheet) to provide practice in listening skills and following oral instructions. If you choose this method, be sure to stop at the end of each direction to allow appropriate time for students to carry out the request. Do NOT repeat any direction, but read each statement slowly and clearly once.

Joker

FOLLOWING DIRECTIONS
(Easy Paper/ Pencil Version)

Purpose: To have fun while learning to follow directions.

Instructions: Divide your paper into six parts. Do this by folding the top down toward the bottom to make two parts, and then folding your paper sideways into three parts. When you open it up, you should have six sections divided by fold-marks. Then carefully follow the directions below.

1. Put your name at the top of the upper left section.

2. Draw a circle in the lower middle section.

3. In the circle, make fifteen dots.

4. In the lower left section, draw a tree upside down.

5. In the top of the tree, draw a bird.

6. Divide the upper right section into three almost equal parts by drawing two horizontal lines.

7. In the top third of the upper right section, put the number *three*.

8. In the lower third of the upper right section, put the letter *H*.

9. Spell *misspell* correctly as you print it sideways (facing the left side of your paper) in the lower right section.

10. Draw three lines under *misspell* and two lines above it.

11. If you feel confused right now, make a big *C*, starting at the upper right corner of your paper, going all the way over to the left side, and ending in the lower right corner.

12. If you think you followed all the directions accurately, make a large *A* beginning in the middle of the top of the top middle section, going down to the lower left section; then beginning again in the top middle section, going down to the lower right section; and finally tracing along the middle fold from left to right between the two sides of your letter.

We will have a student put the correct answers on the chalkboard when you finish. Then you'll be able to see if you know how to follow written directions carefully!

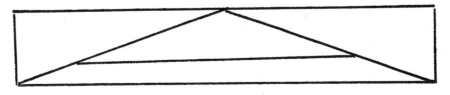

Joker

© 1990 by The Center for Applied Research in Education

Purpose: To see how accurately you can follow written directions.

Instructions: Divide your paper into six almost equal parts. Do this by folding the top down toward the bottom to make two parts and then folding your paper sideways into three parts. When you open it up, you should have six sections divided by fold-marks. Then carefully follow the directions below.

1. Make an *X* in the upper right section of your paper by diagonally marking from the upper right corner to the lower left corner of the section and then diagonally marking from the upper left corner to the lower right corner of the section. In the left triangle of the *X* draw a circle with an *X* inside it.

2. At the bottommost point in the lower middle section of your paper write your name upside down. Underneath your name draw five vertical lines and cross them perpendicularly with one line across the middle.

3. In the upper left section of your paper draw a stick picture of your family. Include all family members. Beneath the picture tell how many people are in your drawing.

4. Divide the lower right section of your paper into five almost equal parts by drawing four horizontal lines. In the top fifth write the first name of the President of the United States. Leave the third and fourth fifth blank. In the second fifth from the top write your middle name with a circle around it. In the bottom fifth print all the vowels.

5. In the upper middle section of your paper print a limerick sideways (facing the left side of your paper). Begin your limerick with, "There once was a young man from Dobbin."

6. In the lower left section of your paper draw five horizontal lines. On the second line, write the plural of *sheep;* on the fourth line, write the singular of *children;* on the first line, write the plural of *lady;* leave the last line blank; on the third line, write the singular of *gentleman.*

7. At the top of the middle bottom section of your paper draw a triangle. Around the triangle draw a circle, but don't let any part of the circle touch the triangle or the fold. On the outer edges of the circle in a circular pattern print your teacher's last name. Put *Mr.,*

Ms., or *Mrs.* in front of it, depending on which is appropriate. Be sure to spell the name correctly.

8. At each innermost intersection of the fold lines draw a square. Trace the fold line between them.

9. If you feel confused right now, make a big *C,* starting at the upper right corner of your paper, going all the way over to the left side of your paper, and ending in the lower right corner.

10. If you think you have followed all the directions accurately, fold your paper up exactly the way you did originally, without reversing any folds, and write *Finished* on the part that is not a flap. Leave it folded on your desk.

11. Let me know when you have finished by raising your hand.

Joker

Purpose: To have fun while learning to follow directions.

Instructions: If you are a boy, start at the last direction and work your way up to the beginning. If you are a girl, begin with the first direction and work your way down to the end. Check off each direction after you have completed it. Do not talk or make any other sounds except those that are included in these directions. (There will be enough activity and commotion.)

1. Go to the window and look out. If you see a car, clap three times; if you don't, make your arms flap like a bird. (Do you feel a bit silly? Never mind.) If you're a boy, you may go to the library to check out a book.

2. Sit down; stand up; sit down; put your head down on your desk; raise your right hand; put your hand on top of your head and pat it while your left hand rubs your tummy. (Not everyone can do this successfully.)

3. Grab a partner (gently) and dance across the room. When you finish, bow to your partner if you are a boy; curtsy to your partner if you are a girl. If you are both girls; stomp your feet twice; if you are both boys, touch your toes. (Come on, guys, you can do it.)

4. Do three jumping jacks; turn halfway around, and do three more. (Isn't this fun?)

5. Hop on one foot to the door, and skip back to your seat, but sit on the floor instead of your chair. (What if our principal walks in right now?)

6. Do five sit-ups; then count to twenty on your fingers while you rest on the floor. (Yes, it'll take twice.)

7. Sit in someone else's seat. (Don't use force!)

8. Walk to the chalkboard pigeon-toed. Return to your seat with toes turned way out. (Remember, if it looks like a duck, it IS a duck!)

9. Hug or shake hands with two students; hug or shake hands with the teacher. (Oh, come on, now. It won't hurt you!)

10. Count the students in the room, and subtract your age from the total. Do this many shoulder circles. (It'll relax you.) If you are a girl, go to the library to check out a book.

INTRO   CASTING SHADOWS

Purpose: To introduce the concept of foreshadowing, such as when an author creates incidents or otherwise provides clues that indicate what will be coming later.

Use personal illustrations. Examples:

When I say, "Take notes on this. You may need the information later," what does this foreshadow? (They will understand that you are giving them a clue that there may be a test later.)

When your parents say, "There's a basketball game tonight, isn't there? You'd better do your homework *now*," what does this foreshadow? (They will pick up the idea that they may not be able to go to the game unless their homework is done.)

From here you can move to literary examples of foreshadowing, or have them read silently a story that includes the technique. Ask them to raise their hand when they think they are getting a clue to later events. Go to their seats and tell them quietly if they're correct or not while the rest continue reading.

Variation: If you prefer, you can have students jot down foreshadowing words as they come to them and discuss the clues as a group later.

JOKER   SURPRISE GUEST

Purpose: To liven up the class; to broaden students' viewpoints by introducing them to a person of ethnic, racial, or social background different from theirs.

Before or after reading a selection involving a culture different from the majority of the students, invite a guest speaker. Prepare the students for the guest so they have enough background to ask appropriate questions about his culture. Be sure the guest is a positive representation of his race, culture, or national heritage. Students enjoy this and learn about themselves in the process.

Follow up the next day, or after the speaker leaves, with a discussion on their feelings about having someone "different" in class. Ask how many had talked personally to a (Hispanic, Black, White, Irishman, Vietnamese, Chinese, rich person, tramp, or whatever) before. Further discussion questions might include:

1. What did they learn about the guest?
2. What did they learn about themselves? (Did they feel different, embarrassed, or uncomfortable in any way?)
3. Would they like to be that person or from that heritage? Why or why not?

INTRO   EXAGGERATION

Purpose: To introduce the concept of hyperbole or exaggeration.

Use personal illustrations, always repeating the pronunciation of the new term. Examples:

I must have told you that a million times! Did I really tell you something that many times? No, I just used hyperbole for effect.

Jerry (use name of student in class) laughed so hard he almost died. Would a person really die from laughing hard? Of course not! Hyperbole was used for effect.

Mary (again, name a student in class) was so happy, her head was in the clouds. Was it really? What was used for effect? (Students will tell YOU, this time.)

JOKER   GOOD DEEDS BOX

Purpose: To build self-worth and self-image; to provide for participation for the common good.

Supply (or have students make) a Good Deeds Box. Fill it with ideas for constructive jobs students can accomplish to improve the appearance or functioning of the classroom.

Examples:

1. Erase the chalkboard.
2. Straighten room library books.
3. Check the desk tops for marks and clean, if needed.
4. Check the floor for scraps of paper or debris and pick up, if needed.
5. Clump out (clean) the erasers.
6. Wash the chalkboard.
7. Go on an errand, if needed.

Students like to help you and to contribute to the group. They will come up with important suggestions of items they think need doing, and you can supply items you would appreciate. Encourage students who are finished with their work to check the Good Deeds Box to draw a suggestion at random and carry out the good deed. Always remember to acknowledge their good deeds!

JOKER   BOOKWORM

Purpose: To build self-image; to encourage reading.

Make a colorful, construction-paper bookworm zig-zag throughout the room (and even down the corridors). Each part of the worm contains the name of a story or book a student has read and the student's name. Connect all the parts to form a very long bookworm.

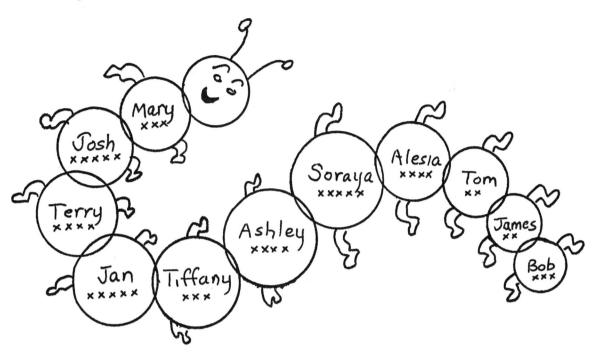

Variation: Use a train with individual cars and call it a booktrain.

Variation: Have students make up an object and give it a catchy name. It could be a gobblety-book (a strange-looking monster of some sort to which names could be added); a long bookbat (a bat with batwings for each segment with names); a bookipede (a centipede with many legs on which to write the names).

INTRO   SENSE APPEAL

Purpose: To introduce students to imagery, the appeal to the senses to arouse emotion and set the mood.

Use examples from their frame of reference. Examples:

You can smell the spicy tomato sauce on the cheese pizza being prepared in the cafeteria. (What image or mental picture do you see? To which senses is the statement appealing?) Let several students describe their images.

We heard the *crrrraaasssh* of metal as the two cars collided. (What image or mental picture do you have? To which senses is the statement appealing?) Again, listen to their descriptions.

Now ask several students to use imagery in sentences. Let them spontaneously create mental pictures appealing to the senses.

It is advisable to move from the concrete experiences of students to the literary work involving the concept. If you begin with the literature and try to explain imagery later, students often miss the point.

INTRO   **JACK AND JILL**

Purpose: To introduce the concept of inference, a conclusion drawn from information given; to show that inferences are not directly stated, but figured out from details supplied.

Copy one of the puzzles on a transparency. Have the projection showing as students enter the room. Omit the answer, of course. This will get their attention, and they will make inferences before you know it!

If it has whiskers, it's a jack or jill.
If it has no nose, it's a jack or jock.
I am thinking of a thing that has whiskers and no nose.
What is it? (Answer: jack)

Older students might be able to tackle this one:

There were three students. One told two lies; one told two truths; one told one lie and one truth.
Terry said: I didn't copy. Mary didn't copy.
Mary said: Terry didn't copy. Shawn copied.
Shawn said: I didn't copy. Terry copied.

Figure out who copied. (Answer: Terry. Mary told two lies; Shawn told two truths; Terry told one lie and one truth.)

Follow with a discussion of the term, *inference,* repeating the word several times. This is a smooth lead-in to a story which requires drawing inferences to be understood.

INTRO   **WILL THE YOUNGEST PLEASE STAND UP?**

Purpose: To introduce a literature selection which involves drawing conclusions or inferences from the information given. This exercise helps develop judgment and reasoning abilities.

Give students ten minutes to answer *yes* or *no* to the inferences. Have them correct their own, and discuss the thinking processes and logic involved in reaching sensible conclusions. Stress that they will need to use the same thought processes to draw logical judgments about the incidents in the story they are about to read. See *YOUNG, OLD, OR IN-BETWEEN*.

Name _____ **Date** _____

Purpose: To try to maintain your concentration and draw logical conclusions.

Instructions: Take a total of ten minutes to answer *yes* or *no* to the inferences below.

1. Sally is older than John; Sally is younger than Pat; therefore Pat is older than John.

2. Sally is younger than Pat; John is older than Pat; therefore John is older than Sally.

3. John is younger than Sally; Pat is younger than John; therefore Sally is older than Pat.

4. Pat is older than Sally; John is younger than Sally; therefore Pat is younger than John.

5. Sally is younger than Pat; Sally is older than John; therefore John is younger than Pat.

6. John is younger than Sally; John is older than Pat; therefore Sally is younger than Pat.

7. Sally is younger than Pat; John is older than Pat; therefore John is younger than Sally.

8. John is older than Pat; Pat is older than Sally; therefore Sally is younger than John.

9. Sally is older than John; John is older than Pat; therefore Sally is older than Pat.

10. Sally is older than John. Pat is older than Sally; therefore Pat is older than John.

JOKER   **LIBRARY TRIP**

Purpose: To encourage outside reading; to acquaint students with local libraries.

Arrange a class trip to the local public library or libraries. If there is a college library, include that, too. Be sure the librarian knows you are coming and can at least conduct a tour. Ask the librarian to explain the organization of books on the shelves, services the library performs, perhaps tell them a story, and (if appropriate) make out library check-out cards for each student.

Many libraries rent pictures, have story-telling times, supply research assistance, rent videotapes, and perform services that may surprise even you. Be certain to prepare students for what they are going to encounter and the behavior standards expected. It is wise to discuss possible questions they could ask to find out more about a library and its functions. Appropriate library behavior should be stressed (quiet atmosphere, book checkout procedure, general courtesy). In addition, a review of card catalog organization and shelving conventions for fiction, nonfiction, and biography can precede the trip.

INTRO   **FIVE-FINGER RULE**

Purpose: To let the student find out for himself if the book or magazine is too difficult for him to read with understanding.

Have the student flip through the book and choose a page at random. He should read one page, putting out one finger every time he doesn't know a word. (Begin with the little finger.) If he reaches his thumb, the book is probably too hard for him to read for pleasure. (The book might be satisfactory for research work if the student is only seeking a small amount of specific information.)

This five-finger rule, though not infallible, is slick because no one needs to know why the student put the book back on the shelf. Each student can check for himself to see if his general reading level is sufficient for the book he chooses.

FOCUS   **CARD CATS**

Purpose: To learn how to find books in the library.

You should bring in at least one box of catalog cards from the library. It is amazing how many students know the information on the cards (as shown in a textbook), but haven't a clue as to what the actual rows of boxes look like! Others cannot locate the boxes when they get to a large library because they don't recognize the huge encasements.

Librarians advise taking students to the library for practical use, rather than spending time in the classroom in artificial situations. The time to learn about the card catalog and Dewey Decimal System is when students need, want, and have the opportunity to find reading material. For minimal classroom necessities, use *CARD CATS* and *LIBRARY LOCATION SKILLS* together.

Focus   ***CARD CATS***

Purpose: To understand the card catalog so you will be able to find any book in the library!

Instructions: Below are three ways to find books in the library. The first and last are easiest.

Remember the CATS.

The   *C*ard Catalog has
       *A*uthor cards,
       *T*itles cards, and
       *S*ubject cards.

- Easy Steps to Find a Book:

  1. Find card catalog.
  2. Decide what to look for (author's last name, title of book, or subject book is about).
  3. Find box containing range of alphabet letters you need.
  4. Locate specific card by looking at TOP LINE of card.
  5. Copy call number on scrap paper (letters and numbers in UPPER LEFT-HAND CORNER of card).
  6. Go to shelves marked with range of numbers and/or letters you need.
  7. Find book according to call number (number and/or letters).

- Another (Harder) Way to Find a Book:

  1. Learn the Dewey Decimal System.
     - 000-099 General Works, including reference works
     - 100-199 Philosophy
     - 200-299 Religion
     - 300-399 Social Sciences
     - 400-499 Language
     - 500-599 Science
     - 600-699 Technology
     - 700-799 The Arts
     - 800-899 Literature
     - 900-999 History

  2. Go to shelves with numbers of subject area you want.
  3. Browse until you find what you need.

- Easy (Computerized) Way to Find a Book:

  1. Find computer.
  2. Decide what to look for (author's last name, title of book, or subject book is about).
  3. Locate specific card by looking at TOP LINE of card.
  4. Copy call number on scrap paper (letters and numbers in UPPER LEFT-HAND CORNER of card).
  5. Go to shelves marked with range of numbers and/or letters you need.
  6. Find book according to call number (number and/or letters).

Purpose: To learn how books are organized in the library so you can always find the books you want.

Fortunately most libraries are organized in similar ways throughout the world. Melvil Dewey, a student in college in the 1800's, devised a system to classify all knowledge into only *ten* categories. This system is called the Dewey Decimal System. You don't have to memorize it to find books in the library, but it is important to know there is such a system. Basics to remember:

1. Similar books are near each other on the bookshelves.

    a. Fiction is together in ALPHABETICAL order (according to author's last name).

    b. Nonfiction is together in NUMERICAL order according to what it is about (subject or topic).

2. Each bookcase is used as one unit.

    a. The alphabet or numbers begin at the top left corner.

    b. The alphabet or numbers snake back and forth in one bookcase unit until they come to the bottom right corner of the cabinet.

    c. The alphabet or numbers continue in the next bookcase, beginning again at the top left corner and snaking.

3. If beginning NUMBERS are the same (332.12 and 332.65), you need to look at first numbers AFTER the decimal. (In this case, the first numbers after the decimals are one and six, so the first numbered book will come before the second one on the shelves.)

4. If beginning LETTERS are the same (Bl and Bl), you need to look at the spines of the books for the author or book you want. (All the Judy Blume books will be together, for example, and books by Blume and Blumf may both be marked with Bl or Blu.)

5. Memorize frequently used categories from Dewey's system:

    000's—references;

    500's—math, earth science, plants, animals;

    700's—arts, photography, music, sports, recreation;

    900's—geography, biography, and history.

6. LEARN TO USE THE CARD CATALOG OR COMPUTERIZED CARD CATALOG.

    This is the easiest way to find a book.

JOKER   SIZZLE

Purpose: To practice saying literary terms; to gain a fuller understanding of definitions of basic literary terminology; to have fun while reinforcing literary concepts; to serve as a review of literary concepts before a test.

This game should be played only after concepts have been introduced or studied. It serves as a fun review to clinch the concepts.

Students play SIZZLE with four teams. Compose questions consisting of factual definitions and examples in three degrees of difficulty (easy, medium, and hard). Students request a question with the degree of difficulty they choose before attempting to answer. The more difficult questions, however, give more degrees (points) for their team toward the winning temperature. Award 10 degrees for answers to easy questions; 20 degrees for medium questions; and 30 degrees for hard questions.

Draw four thermometers on chalkboard (one for each team). These can be very rudimentary sketches. The most important part is to mark each thermometer with lines in 10-degree increments from 0 to 100 degrees.

Students should mark their own number of degrees on the thermometer by coloring in the appropriate area with red chalk after they answer correctly. (You can use regular white or yellow chalk if no red is available, but students like the red best.) An incorrect answer gives 0 degrees. The first team to reach 100 degrees SIZZLES (wins).

This is an easy-to-play, straightforward game. Students do, however, need to prepare by studying the terms and their definitions.

(DO NOT ALLOW STUDENTS TO SEE THE *EXAMPLES* OF THE DEFINITIONS YOU WILL GIVE THEM DURING THE GAME. This allows for surprise, and rewards the ability to *apply* the definitions.)It takes a minimum of thirteen questions before any team can SIZZLE. Usually, it will take longer than this.

See *SIZZLE PREP SHEET* for a reproducible *student* study sheet and SIZZLE EXAMPLES for sample examples for your use as teacher. You can use these examples or make up others appropriate for the age level you are teaching.

Focus   ***SIZZLE PREP SHEET***

Purpose: To provide a study sheet to prepare you for the game of SIZZLE.

Instructions: Study the definitions and be ready to help your team. Your teacher will give the definition and ask you to give the correct literary term. In addition, you will need to identify examples illustrating these literary terms.

10-Point Questions

FORESHADOWING—clues to later events in a story.

FLASHBACK—leaving present time and going to an earlier period.

PLOT—conflict, sequence of events, high point, and conclusion.

POINT OF VIEW—perspective or outlook from which the story is told.

CONFLICT—problem or opposing situation in a story.

CLIMAX—most exciting, high point of the story.

RESOLUTION—conclusion or working-out of the problem in the story.

RHYME—like syllable sounds, usually at the ends of words.

RHYTHM—the cadence of stressed and non-stressed sounds.

MOOD—overall feeling of a literary work.

SETTING—time and place of story.

20-Point Definitions

CONNOTATION—feelings surrounding words.

DENOTATION—dictionary definition of words.

HYPERBOLE—exaggeration for effect.

TONE—author's attitude toward the subject.

METAPHOR—comparison between unlike things.

SIMILE—comparison between unlike things, using *like* or *as*.

ONOMATOPOEIA—words that sound like what they represent.

ALLITERATION—repeated sounds at the beginnings of words.

CHARACTERIZATION—methods used to introduce the people in the story.

SYMBOL—person, event, or object that stands for something else.

IMAGERY—details appealing to senses to arouse emotion or set mood.

INVERSION—subject/predicate reversal for effect.

STEREOTYPE—fixed notion of an individual or group.

THEME—main idea or meaning of a literary work.

30-Point Definitions

INFERENCE—conclusion drawn from information not directly stated.

VERBAL IRONY—difference between what is said and what is meant.

SITUATIONAL IRONY—different twist from what is expected.

DRAMATIC IRONY—reader has information characters don't have.

SATIRE—making fun of vices of society, sometimes to improve it.

PARODY—"take-off" on literary work for humorous effect.

OMNISCIENT POINT OF VIEW—author enters minds of more than one character; story told from all-knowing viewpoint.

1ST PERSON POINT OF VIEW—author enters mind of one character; story sometimes told using "I" as if author is that one character.

3RD PERSON POINT OF VIEW—author reports what characters hear and see as if author is an outside observer; story often uses words like "he," "she," or "it."

Focus   ***SIZZLE EXAMPLES***

Purpose: To provide examples for game of SIZZLE for the *teacher* to use.

Instructions to teacher: IF POSSIBLE, USE EXAMPLES FROM STORIES THE CLASS HAS READ! Each example answered with the correct literary terminology gives 30 degrees on the thermometer. See SIZZLE for how to play the game.

wiggly worm (alliteration)
gobble; screech (onomatopoeia)
The word *sunshine* makes me feel happy. (connotation)
The word *ghost* means "spirit." (denotation)
Displaying a flag might show loyalty. (symbol)
She was a tall, slight, studious girl with a lisp. (characterization)
Her lips were like a rose. (simile)
Her hair was straw. (metaphor)
He fell a million times before he learned to skate. (hyperbole)
It was unlikely he would ever forgive what his friend did to him, and he wanted revenge. (foreshadowing)
The moist hamburger was frying noisily in its grease. (imagery)
The house was dark and the car was gone, so I knew no one was home. (inference)
How very exciting was the book! (inversion)
The main idea of the book was the need for kindness to animals. (theme)
The story was scary and mysterious. (mood)
The author's dislike of animals showed through. (tone)
When the main character was about to drift off, he relived childhood events. (flashback)
To get a laugh, he said I looked beautiful when I was really a mess. (verbal irony)
The story had a surprise ending: she sold her hair to buy him a watch chain, and he sold his watch to buy her a comb. (situational irony)
If the character only knew what we knew, he wouldn't have acted that way. (dramatic irony)
He wanted to go to the beach, but his wife wanted to go to the mountains. (conflict or problem)
Near the end of the book, when she was in the hospital and you didn't know if she'd live or die, you just couldn't put the book down. (climax or high point)
The boys finally worked out their difficulty in the story. (conclusion or resolution)
The narrator said, "I looked at her carefully." (1st person point of view)
The narrator said, "Jeremy looked at them carefully." (3rd person point of view)
The author told us how every one of his characters felt and what they said to each other, so we knew everything that went on. (omniscient point of view)
merry Terry (rhyme)
Texas in the middle of the 1900's (setting)
He dressed his poodle and put him behind the steering wheel of his car, sure that he would be admired. (satire)
To be or not to be a couch potato; that is the question. (parody)
He was boring and wore glasses, just like all the other eggheads. (stereotype)

Note: These examples should not be shown to students. They should use the study sheet (*SIZZLE PREP SHEET*) to prepare themselves for the game of SIZZLE.

INTRO   **ROOM MAG COLLECTION**

Purpose: To collect magazines for student reading, for early finishers, or for use in other class activities.

Encourage students to bring in back issues of magazines for a room collection. Even parents who are reluctant to donate books are usually happy to get rid of magazines.

Place a box or basket in a handy location where students can deposit magazines easily. At first, you will only have a few issues, so you can store them in the basket, and students can return them there when finished reading. Later on, as you gather a larger collection, you can put titles together and store them alphabetically on shelves. This makes it easier for students to find the magazines they like and to replace them for quick use by others.

Often school librarians dispose of older issues (because of storage restraints), and you may be able to become the designated beneficiary. This can add immeasurably to your collection. If your budget allows, it is worthwhile to subscribe to magazines exclusively for your room.

Adult magazines, often not of direct interest to students because of content, can be used for their illustrations for various projects. Useful periodicals geared specifically to young people are *Boy's Life, Writing!, Focus, Science World, National Geographic World, Choices, Career World, 3-2-1 Contact, Young Miss, Bananas, Ebony, Jr., Cricket, Ranger Rick, Penny Power, Games, Junior, Odyssey, Sports Illustrated for Kids,* and various *Scholastic Magazine* editions. *National Geographic, Teen, Seventeen, National Wildlife, Hispanic, Life, Sports Illustrated, People, Time, U.S. News and World Report, BMX Plus, Sport, Consumer Reports, Ski, Skiing,* and other specialized trade magazines on sports, computers, and hobbies are also popular.

FOCUS   **MAGAZINE SUMMARY**

Purpose: To use as a check-up on student reading of magazine articles; to give practice in picking out main ideas; to encourage student reactions to reading materials.

Middle school students often prefer magazines to books. They like the format of short articles and highly illustrative material, and appreciate topics written directly for their age and reading levels. Encouraging and giving recognition to magazine reading is one way to spur students to read on diversified topics, and to capture the interest of reluctant readers. By requiring reaction to what is read, you give them a chance to express their own views and show them you are interested in what they think.

School libraries have subscriptions to many magazines appropriate for young readers, and students subscribe to hobby, car, teen, sport, and other reading they enjoy. You may have to screen the magazines a bit, as there are magazines of questionable literary worth on the market, but usually students choose wisely, and you may even be introduced to a few technical or specialized magazines with which you are unfamiliar. For a possible report form for students to use to report their magazine reading, see *MAGAZINE SUMMARY*.

Focus ***MAGAZINE SUMMARY***

Instructions: Summarize (give the main ideas) of the magazine article. At the end give your reactions to what you read. Do you agree, disagree, believe, or disbelieve? How do you feel about the topic as presented?

Name_____ **Date**_____

NAME OF MAGAZINE_____MAG DATE_____

NAME OF ARTICLE _____

TOPIC _____NUMBER OF PAGES_____

IN ONE PARAGRAPH SUMMARIZE MAIN POINTS:

_____

_____

_____

_____

_____

_____

_____

_____

YOUR REACTIONS TO WHAT YOU READ:

_____

_____

_____

_____

_____

_____

_____

_____

What I Think

INTRO AND FOCUS   **HEADLINES**

Purpose: To introduce and practice picking out the main ideas while reading.

Read several short newspaper articles to your class (or have volunteers read them aloud). Ask students to make up headlines, and point out the relationship between the headlines and articles. Be sure they understand that the headline captures interest and also includes the main idea. Follow by having students put a headline on selections they read.

Variation: Have each student cut out a short newspaper article, snip off the headline, and put both face-down on his desk. Ask for volunteers to read their articles (omitting the headlines), and have the others make up appropriate "main idea" headlines. Compare student-created headlines with the actual newspaper headlines and discuss.

INTRO AND FOCUS   **NOTE-TAKING**

Purpose: To introduce three ways to take notes efficiently (webbing, outline, and box systems); to provide an organized way to show main ideas and subordinate details.

Begin with an explanation of three ways to find the main ideas and put them down on paper. Point out that they are all similar since the same ideas will be the main ones no matter which method they choose.

Explain WEBBING and pass out copies of *CATS*. Follow up by having them outline or use the box system on the same article, or assign other writing for them to outline or box.

FOCUS   **WEBBING**

Purpose: To learn to pick out main ideas and categorize details.

Give students any informational writing to read. Have them take notes on the main ideas using a technique called webbing.

Webbing is an efficient form of note-taking. As students read, they put down an idea and draw a circle around it. It is best to start in the middle of the page because the web will grow like a spider web from the focal point (central idea) to the outer edges (details).

As students reach the next idea they want to remember, they jot down a word (not more than two!) and circle it. They also need to connect it to another idea on their sheet. This procedure does wonders for organizing thoughts and keeping students from copying verbatim from the text.

Variation: Make an overhead transparency showing webbing of a story or informational article. Discuss the relationships between the parts of the web.

Variation: Webs can be made with lines only (no circles).

Distribute *CATS* to provide practice in using a web as a note-taking technique for informational writing.

Focus   *CATS*

Name_____   Date_____

Purpose: To learn to pick out main ideas and categorize details.

Instructions: You are going to use webbing as a method of note-taking. Put main ideas or concepts toward the middle of your paper in large circles. Then branch out with smaller circles as you find details belonging to the main ideas. Attach this sheet to your web.

CATS

There are many different kinds of cats, but most popular are Siamese, Persian, and plain alley cats. All these cats have retractable claws, excellent hearing, and outstanding vision (especially at night), but there are differences, too.

Siamese are short-haired cats with wiry, strong bodies. They like to climb up into high places, and when they don't get their way, they let their owners know with piercing, distinctive voices.

Persian cats are long-haired. They have squashed-in faces with short noses. They are very soft and full-bodied.

Alley cats are of mixed breeding. They can be any color, size, or shape, depending upon their mixture. Some people think alley cats are healthier and better mousers because they have to fend for themselves in the streets.

All cats need love, attention, food, and water to grow properly and be pleasant pets. Exercise is important, too, for cats can get too fat just as people can.

PRACTICE YOUR WEB ON THE BACK OF THIS SHEET. MAKE A *NEAT* NOTE-TAKING WEB ON YOUR OWN PAPER.

Focus   ***NOTE-TAKING* (Outline System)**

Name_____   Date_____

I. _____   VI. _____

   A. _____   A. _____

   B. _____   B. _____

   C. _____   C. _____

   D. _____   D. _____

II. _____   VII. _____

   A. _____   A. _____

   B. _____   B. _____

   C. _____   C. _____

   D. _____   D. _____

III. _____   VIII. _____

   A. _____   A. _____

   B. _____   B. _____

   C. _____   C. _____

   D. _____   D. _____

IV. _____   IX. _____

   A. _____   A. _____

   B. _____   B. _____

   C. _____   C. _____

   D. _____   D. _____

V. _____   X. _____

   A. _____   A. _____

   B. _____   B. _____

   C. _____   C. _____

Focus *NOTE-TAKING* (Box System)

Name_____ Date_____

Details	Main Ideas	Details

_____

_____

_____

_____

_____

_____

_____

_____

_____

_____

_____

_____

_____

_____

_____

_____

_____

_____

Focus   *POETRY MAP*

Name_____ Date_____

TITLE OF POEM _____

POET _____

POINT OF VIEW _____

TO WHOM IS THE PERSON SPEAKING? _____

SETTING _____

EVENTS, IF NARRATIVE _____

_____

_____

MOOD _____

WORDS THAT INVOKE FEELINGS

WORD_____ FEELING_____

WORD_____ FEELING_____

WORD_____ FEELING_____

WORDS THAT REPEAT SOUNDS

WORD_____ SOUND_____

WORD_____ SOUND_____

WORD_____ SOUND_____

WORDS THAT CREATE IMAGES

WORD_____ SENSE APPEALED TO_____

WORD_____ SENSE APPEALED TO_____

WORD_____ SENSE APPEALED TO_____

WHAT DID YOU LIKE BEST ABOUT THIS POEM? _____

FOCUS   **POETRY READING**

Purpose: To become more at ease reading poetry orally; to practice interpreting the mood poetry creates.

Instructions to students: Choose a narrative poem you like. Read and rehearse it. Copy it out on note cards (one side). Give the title and poet, and read the poem with expression to the class.

Variation: Choose a poem which shows emotion. Create the mood with music, a painting, sculpture, costume, or other means. Copy the poem on note cards (one side) or memorize to recite for the class. Be sure to give title and poet before beginning.

Variation: Write an original poem and proceed as above.

INTRO   **RHYME TIME**

Purpose: To introduce the concept and sound of rhyming words.

Put one of the following groups of words across the top of the chalkboard, leaving room for words to be written underneath each. Students come up one at a time and write a rhyming word under the lead word. Each student should read aloud his column of words from top to bottom to reinforce sounds.

Easy-to-rhyme groups of words:

      and, it, ill, sing, old
      right, can, mail, in, sat
      say, book, lake, damp, bang

INTRO   **INCOMPLETE RHYMES**

Purpose: To introduce the concept and sound of rhyming words; to induce active participation before studying rhyme.

Read sentences or phrases and have students complete them orally. They will say them (sometimes loudly!) in unison back to you.

Examples:

1. I had a cat that was very _____.
2. I went to the door and fell on the _____.
3. The phone can't sing, but it can _____.
4. For heaven's sake, don't fall in the _____.
5. I put my mail into a _____.
6. He's out of sight, but that's all _____.
7. I took the soup out of the can, and put it all into the _____.
8. Bert and Jill went up the _____.
9. I have the book, but please don't _____.
10. When a picture I tried to hang, I hit my thumb with an awful _____.
11. Whenever they tell the story of old, the rainbow ends with a pot of _____.
12. What will it take to bake a _____?
13. It's dark all right in the middle of the _____?
14. Make the report, not long, but _____.
15. This ends the rhyme; we're out of _____.

ADD-A-LETTER RHYME

Name_____   Date_____

Purpose: To practice making larger words rhyme.

Instructions: Add letters at the beginning of the key letters to form rhyming words. You may use the dictionary to check spellings or for ideas.

1. _____action

   _____

   _____

   _____

2. _____ation

   _____

   _____

   _____

3. _____otion

   _____

   _____

   _____

4. _____aunch

   _____

   _____

   _____

5. _____ology

   _____

   _____

6. _____ealer

   _____

   _____

   _____

7. _____ancer

   _____

   _____

   _____

8. _____ection

   _____

   _____

   _____

9. _____obble

   _____

   _____

   _____

10. _____rawl

   _____

   _____

Focus *RESEARCH FLOW CHART*

Purpose: To show basic research process from start to finish.

Instructions: Begin at START and flow downward to STOP to keep yourself on track during your research.

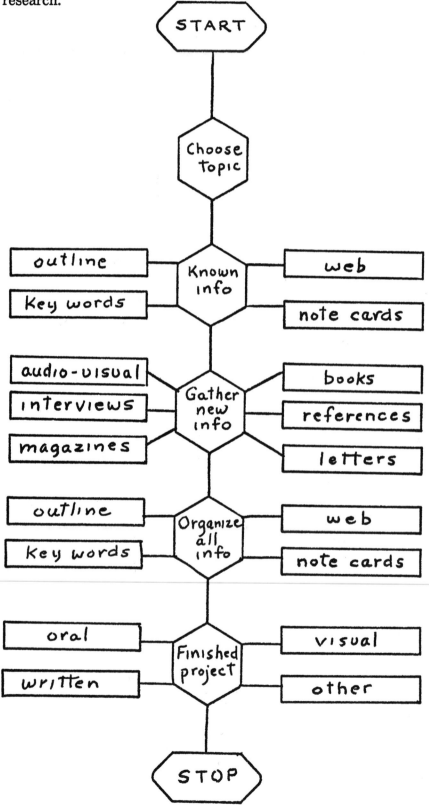

Purpose: To show main ways to report your research project.

Instructions: This report web should be read from the largest circles outward. It can help you decide on an appropriate method of reporting the information you gather.

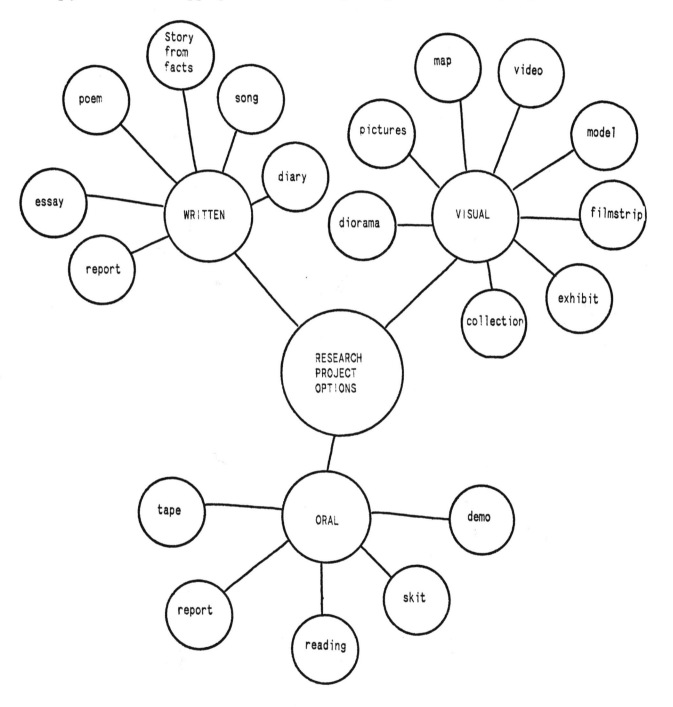

FOCUS   **REPORTING ON RESEARCH**

Purpose: To provide alternatives to basic research reports.

1. As a class project, research a broad topic. Have students enter the information and facts discovered into a computer data base.

Students can then use the data base to find answers to questions you supply (or they want to find out). Students can use the sort and search features of their software to find specific answers and to compare or contrast aspects of their topic.

2. If research is historical (and applicable), have students report by making a chronological time line.

3. If research is ethnic, have students create a mural depicting the culture or contrasting two cultures.

4. Ask students to prepare a game to test the information included in their research report. (This game could be a computer game.)

JOKER   **ONE DAY AT A TIME**

Purpose: To provide an ongoing literary experience; to provide enjoyment.

Always have a story in progress; that is, read orally to the students an outstanding book or story in segments. You can use those extra minutes that occur when everyone is finished with their work or the school schedule changes.

Letting students vote on what you will read to them (after you introduce several stories you recommend) helps assure attentiveness. Any of the following books (all awarded the Newbery Medal) offer insight and knowledge, as well as entertainment:

THE VOYAGES OF DR. DOOLITTLE by Lofting
THE CAT WHO WENT TO HEAVEN by Coatsworth
THE WHITE STAG by Seredy
CALL IT COURAGE by Sperry
THE DOOR IN THE WALL by De Angeli
. . . AND NOW MIGUEL by Krumgold
ISLAND OF THE BLUE DOLPHINS by O'Dell
A WRINKLE IN TIME by L'Engle
I, JUAN DE PAREJA by de Trevino
FROM THE MIXED-UP FILES OF MRS. BASIL E. FRANKWEILER
     by Koingsburg
SOUNDER by Armstrong
MRS. FRISBEE AND THE RATS OF NIMH by O'Brien
JULIE OF THE WOLVES by George
BRIDGE TO TERABITHIA by Paterson
DICEY'S SONG by Voigt
THE WHIPPING BOY by Fleischman

Variation: Students sometimes prefer to have the better readers in the class

Purpose: To have fun with metaphors and similes.

Instructions: Take ten minutes to prepare a pantomime or skit to illustrate one of the following similes or metaphors. If you prefer, draw a picture showing the figure of speech being taken literally.

Example: **The girl plowed through her room.** You would draw an actual farmer's plow with the girl behind it literally plowing her way through her room.

1. Marsha became a cheetah, first down on her haunches observing, but springing suddenly with force and swiftness to claw her assailant.

2. Once the first book was pushed, the rest toppled one by one to the floor like a row of dominoes.

3. The typewriter was a tap dancer, its rhythms varied and pleasant.

4. The car skidded on the ice as if it were being driven on (butter) (banana peels).

5. Her eyes were (saucers) (emeralds) (tiny, brown beads).

6. His hair is like (porcupine quills) (carrots) (a rainbow).

7. Her lips were a (velvety rose) (hamburger) (pencil line).

8. His nerves were (hammers pounding) (short-circuited wires) inside his head.

9. The sunrise spread over the landscape like a fiery octopus stretching its tentacles in every direction.

10. The children were animated bees, buzzing and darting around the guest flower.

IF YOU HAVE TIME, YOU CAN CHOOSE MORE THAN ONE OPTION. YOU MAY NEED OTHER STUDENTS TO HELP YOU ACT OUT SOME OF THESE FIGURES OF SPEECH, BUT YOUR DRAWINGS SHOULD BE DONE ALONE.

take turns reading. This allows for voice variety and image-building. (You can't assume you are the "best" reader or have the most expressive voice!)

Variation: Students like to doodle or draw while listening. If the reading session is lengthy (fifteen minutes or more), encourage them to draw the characters, setting, or events. If some students prefer abstract doodling, fine.

FOCUS   SKIM THE NEWS

Purpose: To practice the skill of skimming.

Pass out one page of newspaper to each student. Be sure these are written pages, not primarily illustrations. Tell pupils to skim the articles and assimilate as much as they can as quickly as they can. Emphasize they are not to "read" the paper, but to skim quickly through it as fast as possible.

Give a time limit depending on the general reading level of the group. Two or three minutes is right for most. At the end of the time limit, have students take out a piece of paper and list as many ideas or facts as they can without looking back at the newspaper pages.

Variation: Distribute two sides of one page of a periodical, and proceed as above.

FOCUS   SPEED READ

Purpose: To practice reading quickly.

Give a short clipping to each student. Allow thirty seconds to read it. Have each student write a summary of their clipping.

Variation: Copy an article on an overhead transparency. Show it for thirty seconds. Have each student write a summary of the article.

Variation: Give a newspaper page to each student. Have them check headlines only. Allow thirty seconds. Have them list as many headlines as they can. Allow use of their own words as long as they have the gist of the headline.

Variation: Divide an article or story into logical phrases. Have students practice reading swiftly within a time limit. You may want to provide three stories to accommodate different reading speeds in the class. Students could then choose the short, medium, or long article. This way students can try speed reading more than once to increase their speed and advance to the longer articles.

Do NOT wait for everyone to finish. Challenge even your best readers. For an example of an article written in phrases, see *SPEEDY READERS*.

Focus   *SPEEDY READERS*

Purpose: To help you speed up reading by reading in phrases.

Instructions: Read this as quickly as you can. Your time is limited. You will summarize what you have read.

COMPUTERS

Computers are   very complex   and helpful machines.

They can do   numerous things   to make our jobs easier,

especially tasks   that require   lots of repetition.

Some of the jobs   they excel in   are alphabetizing,

carrying out formulas,   sorting,   editing,   and graphics.

Of course,   man must make   the computer run.

The computer is   only as good   as the operator.

As someone once said,   GIGO.   That stands for

"Garbage in;   garbage out!"   It means that

if the computer operator   puts in nonsense

or wrong information,   the computer   can only put out

misinformation and junk.

So never spend   any of your time   blaming the computer

when it doesn't work right.   In almost every case,

it is the person   who is operating the computer

that has "goofed."

Almost every job   requires knowledge of computers.

The sales clerk   in the store,   the airline worker,

the secretary,   the bookkeeper,   the store owner,

gas station attendant—   all these use computers

on a daily basis.   If you want to succeed

in the information generation,   you will have to learn

more about computers.

INTRO   **STUDENT TIME LINE**

Purpose: To build self-image; to introduce the idea of a time line to show chronological order.

Have students make a time line (in months insteads of years) with pictures of students along the time line in order of birth. This simple project instills the concept of a time line and is a good activity to precede a story which needs to be put in chronological order historically.

The student time line can be placed at the top or bottom of a large bulletin board space. This way other items can also be displayed on the bulletin board at the same time. The pictured time line can remain for most of the year if desired.

Section III

WORDS AND SENTENCES

LIST OF COMMON ABBREVIATIONS

Instructions: Use this list to study abbreviations in common use. Use as a resource for assignments.

A.D.–*Anno Domini* (Latin)–in the year of our Lord
a.m.–*ante meridiem* (Latin)–before noon
ad. lib.–*ad libitum* (Latin)–at pleasure (when you want)
adj.–adjective
adv.–adverb
anon.–anonymous
ans.–answer
app.–appendix
arith.–arithmetic
Ave.–Avenue
B.C.–before Christ; also British Columbia
biog.–biography
cap.–capital
cat.–catalog
ch. or chs.–chapter or chapters
cm.–centimeter
Col.–Colonel
conj.–conjunction
Corp.–Corporal
cu. or cub.–cubic
Mon., Tues., Wed., Thurs., Fri., Sat., Sun.–days of week.
der. or deriv.–derivation
doz.–dozen
Dr.–Doctor
e.g.–*exempli gratia* (Latin)–for example

ea.–each
et al.–*et alibi* (Latin)–and elsewhere; also *et alii* (Latin)–and others
etc.–*et cetera* (Latin)–and so forth
f.o.b.–free on board—no charge for shipping
Fahr.–Fahrenheit
fict.–fiction
ft.–foot or feet
gaz.–gazetteer
gram.–grammar
hist.–history
in.–inch
interj.–interjection
kg.–kilogram
km.–kilometer
lb. or lbs.–pound or pounds
lib.–library
LP–long playing record
M.D.–Doctor of Medicine
m.p.h.–miles per hour
Mad.–Madam
Maj.–Major
math.–mathematics
max.–maximum
mg.–milligram
Mr.–Mister
mm.–millimeter
Jan., Feb., Mar., Apr., May, June, July, Aug., Sept., Oct., Nov., Dec.–months
Mrs.–title for married lady
Ms.–title for married or unmarried lady
no. or nos.–number or numbers
num.–numbers
oz.–ounce or ounces
p. and pp.–page and pages
p.m.–*post meridiem* (Latin)–afternoon
P.O.–Post Office
P.S.–*postscriptum* (Latin)–postscript
pen.–peninsula
pers.–person
pl.–plural
prep.–preposition
pron.–pronoun
pseud.–pseudonym (false name)
pt.–pint

qt.–quart
R.S.V.P.–*Repondez, s'il vous plait* (French)–Reply, if you please
rad.–radical
rec.–record
ref.–reference
Rev.–Reverend
sci.–science
Sgt.–Sergeant
sing.–singular
soc.–society
Sr.–Senior
St.–street or saint
syn.–synonym
tel.–telephone
v.–verb
vol. and vols.–volume and volumes
vs.–versus (opposing)
yd. and yds.–yard and yards
yr. and yrs.–year and years

Focus   ***ABOMINABLE ABBREVIATIONS***

Name_____   Date_____

Purpose: To have fun with abbreviations; to sharpen recall of commonly used abbreviations; to figure out homophones or words that nearly sound alike.

Instructions: Find the abbreviation for each italicized word. Then discover the word that the abbreviation makes or a word that sounds like the abbreviation. Example: *Arizona* is italicized. The abbreviation is AZ. It sounds like *as.*

Substitute words with the sounds of the abbreviated words in the sentences. Rewrite the sentences so they make sense.

1. *Wyoming* don't you *Colonel* and *telephone* her I left my *peninsula* and *person* where I *Saturday?*

_____

2 The *catalog history* at *Maine* as I tried to *Friday inch* the *Sunday.*

_____

3. *January* was *Madam* because *maximum* stepped on the *gazetteer* and let his engine *Reverend.*

_____

4. "*Number* way will I *Wednesday* you! *Dozen* that sound like women's *library?*" she asked with a *science.* She *pseudonym* him instead!

_____

5. I'm a *record.* My *numbers* is sore; my fingers are *number;* and my eyesight is only *Fahrenheit.*

_____

6. I put on my *society* and *capital Arizona* I began to *singular.*

_____

7. *Massachusetts* and *Pennsylvania* said *Alabama* was *Illinois.*

_____

8. *Idaho* like to say "*Hawaii*" to my *answer,* but *Wyoming, Ohio, Wisconsin,* did they *synonym?*

_____

ABBREVIATION VARIATION

Name_____ Date_____

Purpose: To have fun with abbreviations; to sharpen recall of commonly used abbreviations; to have fun with homophones.

Instructions: Make a list of all abbreviations used. After the abbreviation, put the word for which the abbreviation stands. There are a total of 42 abbreviations.

1. WY don't you Col. and tel. her I left my pen. and pers. where I Sat.?
2. The cat. hist. at Me. AZ I tried to Fri. in. the Sun..
3. Jan. was Mad. because max. stepped on the gaz. and let his engine Rev..
4. "No. way will I Wed. you! Doz. that sound like women's lib.?" she asked with a sci.. She pseud. him instead.
5. I'm a rec.. My nos. is sore; my cheeks are num.; and my eyesight is only Fahr..
6. I put on my soc. and cap. and began to sing..
7. MA and PA said AL was IL.
8. ID like to say HI to my ans., but WY, OH, WI did they syn.?

1. _____	22. _____	
2. _____	23. _____	
3. _____	24. _____	
4. _____	25. _____	
5. _____	26. _____	
6. _____	27. _____	
7. _____	28. _____	
8. _____	29. _____	
9. _____	30. _____	
10. _____	31. _____	
11. _____	32. _____	
12. _____	33. _____	
13. _____	34. _____	
14. _____	35. _____	
15. _____	36. _____	
16. _____	37. _____	
17. _____	38. _____	
18. _____	39. _____	
19. _____	40. _____	
20. _____	41. _____	
21. _____	42. _____	

Name_____ **Date**_____

Purpose: To practice using abbreviations of states of the United States using postal designations; to get used to using capital letters with no periods for these two-letter state abbreviations.

Instructions: Print postal abbreviations on the correct states on the map. You may consult an encyclopedia, atlas, or other reference, if needed.

AL	ALABAMA	MT	MONTANA
AK	ALASKA	NE	NEBRASKA
AZ	ARIZONA	NV	NEVADA
AR	ARKANSAS	NH	NEW HAMPSHIRE
CA	CALIFORNIA	NJ	NEW JERSEY
CO	COLORADO	NM	NEW MEXICO
CT	CONNECTICUT	NY	NEW YORK
DE	DELAWARE	NC	NORTH CAROLINA
FL	FLORIDA	ND	NORTH DAKOTA
GA	GEORGIA	OH	OHIO
HI	HAWAII	OK	OKLAHOMA
ID	IDAHO	OR	OREGON
IL	ILLINOIS	PA	PENNSYLVANIA
IN	INDIANA	RI	RHODE ISLAND
IA	IOWA	SC	SOUTH CAROLINA
KS	KANSAS	SD	SOUTH DAKOTA
KY	KENTUCKY	TN	TENNESSEE
LA	LOUISIANA	TX	TEXAS
ME	MAINE	UT	UTAH
MD	MARYLAND	VT	VERMONT
MA	MASSACHUSETTS	VA	VIRGINIA
MI	MICHIGAN	WA	WASHINGTON
MN	MINNESOTA	WV	WEST VIRGINIA
MS	MISSISSIPPI	WI	WISCONSIN
MO	MISSOURI	WY	WYOMING

JOKER   FAST AFFIXES

Purpose: To give practice in forming words by adding prefixes or suffixes to the root (stem).

Put common prefixes, roots, and suffixes on chalkboard in columns. Also, have four blank columns labelled Team I, Team II, Team III, and so on.

First member of Team I comes quickly to the chalkboard, draws lines connecting any root with any prefix, suffix, or both prefix and suffix. He then writes the completed word on the board under his team's column. First member of Team II does the same. The lines show the next participants which ones have been used. The list of newly formed words is a double-check (in case the crossing lines get confusing), a visual learning aid to those waiting their turns, and a running score-card to see which team is ahead.

This game works well on a timed basis, and moves along quickly to hold student interest. Give each student no longer than 20 seconds to finish his turn. Allowing ten minutes for the entire game is sufficient for most classes since students can figure out their words ahead of their turn. If someone else uses their word first, they will have to think of another! The team with the most new words CORRECTLY SPELLED when time is up is the winner. If a student is drawing lines when time is called, he must sit down without putting his word in the column for his team. If he has completed his lines, however, or is in the process of writing his new word, he should be allowed to complete his turn.

INTRO   GUESS THE PREFIX OR SUFFIX

Purpose: To introduce prefixes and suffixes by using deductive reasoning; to introduce further study of affixes.

Put a series of words with the same prefix (and/or suffix) on a transparency for the overhead projector. Have them deduce the prefix or affix meaning.

Example:	re	gain	Example:	state	ment
	re	teach		place	ment
	re	do		argue	ment
	re	view		entertain	ment
	re	trace		amaze	ment
	re	instate		encircle	ment

They will easily see that *re* means *again.*

Students will deduce that *ment* is added to an action to name the thing (noun) that these action verbs represent. (You *state* something; what you state is called a *statement.*)

Variation: Make copies of the ready-made list of examples in *GUESS THE AFFIX*. Students will not get exact meanings for all affixes, but discussion of guesses is important.

Focus   *GUESS THE AFFIX*

Name_____ **Date**_____

Purpose: To learn the terms, affix, prefix, and suffix.

Instructions: An affix is a prefix or suffix. A PREFIX is added to the main part of the word at the BEGINNING. A SUFFIX is added to the main part of the word at the END. Guess what the affixes mean, based on your knowledge of the words.

Prefixes at Beginning

un aided
un alike   un means _____
un anchored

pre game
pre test   pre means _____
pre school

in active
in destructible   in means _____
in expensive

sub marine
sub arctic   sub means _____
sub group

mis spell
mis speak   mis means _____
mis lead

Suffixes at End

mother hood
child hood   hood means _____
state hood

commun ism
critic ism   ism means _____
alcohol ism

smooth ness
rough ness   ness means _____
cheerful ness

tooth less
penni less   less means _____
child less

attend ant
cool ant   ant means _____
account ant

Focus　　　　　　*COMMON ROOTS AND AFFIXES*

Name_____　Date_____

Purpose: To practice making new words by adding affixes.

Instructions: See how many new words you can make by connecting any root with a prefix, suffix, or both. Then write the completed new words below. You may use the dictionary to check spellings. Only properly spelled words will be counted as correct.

Prefix	*Roots*	*Suffix*
un (not)	joy	ness (state of)
re (back or again)	move	ance (state of)
pre (before)	heat	hood (state of)
in (into)	view	er (that does)
in (not)	kind	ant (that does)
en (in)	script	able (can be)
de (from)	form	ful (full of)
sub (under)	treat	ous (full of)
pro (in front of)	program	ish (like)
over (over)	use	ly (like)
mis (wrongly)	friend	ment (act of)
dis (opposite of)	child	ion (act of)
per (through)	tract	less (without)

_____ _____ _____ _____

_____ _____ _____ _____

_____ _____ _____ _____

_____ _____ _____ _____

_____ _____ _____ _____

_____ _____ _____ _____

_____ _____ _____ _____

_____ _____ _____ _____

_____ _____ _____ _____

_____ _____ _____ _____

_____ _____ _____ _____

_____ _____ _____ _____

FOCUS   **CLASS ALPHABET**

Purpose: To practice alphabetizing, using words from their personal experiences.

Run off a list of class members' first and last names NOT in alphabetical order. Have students alphabetize all the first names in one column and the last names in another. Have them see how many (if any) people are in the exact same position alphabetically with both first and last names. Example:

Tom Martin
Terry Bobo
Robin Friend

would result in the following lists:

Robin   Bobo
Terry   Friend
Tom   Martin

Thus, Tom was the only student in the same order on both lists. The students revel in seeing who is opposite their names!

FOCUS   **ROOM ALPHABET**

Purpose: To practice alphabetizing using words from their personal experiences; to have fun alphabetizing.

Instructions to students: Alphabetize words from the room that begin with the same letter as your first, middle, or last names. You may look inside purses, desks, drawers, and other places (with permission) to find more items.

Give students the choice of names because if *Z* or *Q* is a first letter, it would be difficult to find enough items. Example: Xavier Zeb Perry would be better off with his last name. After making their list, students should put the list in alphabetical order.

You can place a minimum and/or maximum number of items for the list to keep the class almost together as far as time expended. A reasonable guide would be ten to twenty items. Remember, the main idea is to get them alphabetizing. Lists should be shared.

Variation: Instead of general objects, use room books, textbooks, teachers' names, school subjects, or street names where classmates live.

ANAGRAM ANOMALY

Name_____ **Date**_____

Purpose: To have fun with words; to teach what an anagram is; to arouse curiosity and interest in word patterns.

Instructions: An anagram is a word that is formed by transposing the letters of another word. Find words in the following brief paragraph that can be rearranged into new words. There are ten. Write both the original word and its anagram on the same line. Example: *arm = mar* or *ram.*

The vile monster laid his instrument down and took out the reed. The teacher saw him cheat. "Oh, dear!" he said. "I'm in trouble now."

1. _____

2. _____

3. _____

4. _____

5. _____

6. _____

7. _____

8. _____

9. _____

10. _____

You can use the space below to practice and try out words.

Joker   ***CAN A CAT BECOME A DOG?***

Name_____ **Date**_____

Purpose: To have fun with anagrams; to develop logical thinking skills; to learn what an anagram is.

Instructions: Change one letter at a time, keeping all the other letters the same. See if you can make a cat become a dog; a boy become a man; hate become love, etc. Use only the number of steps shown.

1. CAP

    ———

    HAT

2. LIKE

    ———

    LOVE

3. MOUSE

    ———

    HORSE

4. BOY

    ———

    ———

    MAN

5. CAT

    ———

    ———

    DOG

6. RAIN

    ———

    HAIL

7. POP

    ———

    ———

    TEA

8. GOAT

    ———

    ———

    BEAR

9. HATE

    ———

    ———

    ———

    LOVE

10. FOUL

    ———

    ———

    FAIR

Can you make up an anagram?

    ———

    ———

    ———

    ———

GETTING ACQUAINTED WITH ANTONYMS

Name_____   Date_____

Purpose: To introduce a lesson on antonyms; to review known opposites before tackling harder ones.

Instructions: Add one letter to each word to form word pairs which are antonyms (opposites). Example: *(s)*it stand

_____own	up	_____other	father
_____each	_____earn	_____eat	_____old
tin_____	hug_____	_____right	_____ark
whit_____	_____lack	_____omen	me_____
_____part	together	_____anger	safety
_____all	rise	man_____	few
_____pen	_____lose	_____ate	love
_____ought	_____old	_____all	short
scow_____	_____mile	lad_____	gentleman
_____ear	men_____	_____our	sweet

Focus   ***GETTING BRANDED***

Name_____   **Date** _____

Purpose: To emphasize the difference between a product and a brand name; to show that only brand names are capitalized.

Instructions: Copy the brand name before the general category of product. Use every word in the list.

Example: Cheerios cereal (Brand name capitalized; general term not.)

adhesive

apple   1. _____

band aid

bic   2. _____

bicycle

bold   3. _____

book

bottle   4. _____

camera

car   5. _____

coke

computer   6. _____

copier

dishwashing liquid   7. _____

detergent

ford   8. _____

gem

general electric   9. _____

harley-davidson

ivory   10. _____

jeans

joy   11. _____

kodak

levi   12. _____

GETTING BRANDED (Continued)

motorcycle

notebook — 13. ______________________

paper clips

pen — 14. ______________________

prell

prentice hall — 15. ______________________

refrigerator

royal — 16. ______________________

schwinn

scott — 17. ______________________

shampoo

soap — 18. ______________________

tissue

trapper keeper — 19. ______________________

typewriter

xerox — 20. ______________________

Focus   ***CONNOTATION CONNECTIONS***

Name_____ Date_____

Purpose: To show that a connotation is a feeling connected to a word, as opposed to the literal meaning of the word.

Instructions: See what your FEELINGS tell you. The words in parentheses mean the same. Circle your preference in each pair. We will discuss the connotations when you finish.

Which would you rather be?

1. I would rather be (thin, skinny).

2. I would rather be (obese, heavy).

3. I would rather be (perfect, undeformed).

4. I would rather be (dull, inactive).

5. I would rather be (prosperous, filthy rich).

6. I would rather be (an intelligent person, an egghead).

7. I would rather be a (custodian, janitor).

8. I would rather be a (sanitation worker, garbage collector).

9. I would rather live in a (crackerbox, small house).

10. I would rather own a/an (old car, jalopy).

11. I would rather have a sweater that is (cheap, inexpensive).

12. I would rather have a dog that is (a mongrel, of mixed breed).

13. I would rather have (a Popsicle, frozen sweetened water).

14. I would rather wear (spectacles, glasses).

15. I would rather have a nose that is (prominent, large).

16. I would rather be (shy, fearful).

17. I would rather be (stubborn, pig-headed).

18. I would rather be (confident, cocky).

19. I would rather be (harebrained, reckless).

20. I would rather be (vulgar, in poor taste).

Joker   *CAN YOU DE-CODE DE CODE?*

Name _____   Date _____

Purpose: To develop reasoning power; to have fun with letters and words; to develop perception skills; to learn what a cryptogram is; to decode a cryptogram.

Instructions: A cryptogram is a coded message. Find the three proverbs hidden in the cryptograms below by crossing out unnecessary, extra letters. See *PROVERBIAL TRUTHS* for a list of proverbs to guide you.

TTHESEWIHLEOLLSAUQPTGUHSSILNXASPBCTILQAOOPUSDGKJGHS OOZZBOXEASPT.

_____

_____

QWEYASFOJHUMZCSDAPIYDEPKNLSSAQQY,BOOUIITTMVNCINVMIW EWIPPLYIXLNPOT.

_____

_____

SQWEPAJHURKNNBETPIHIDECNNRKKOHSDAKNJDSPILOEILSSTWHQ PPENCKHUSAILXD.

_____

_____

Instructions: If you can de-code the following message, you may do what it says! To crack the code, you need to substitute letters for other letters. HINT: In this puzzle *a* has been substituted for *y*. The same letter will be substituted every time. There have been six other substitutions of letters made.

Aco zaa lxavx thx pccz, gxt a dpilk, ald gc tc thx pxst pccz.

_____

If you wish, make up a coded message on the line below.

_____

Name _____ **Date** _____

Purpose: To have fun while using reasoning powers to figure out word puzzle answers.

Instructions: The following well-known poem has its vowels left out. See if you can reconstruct the poem correctly by inserting the missing vowels (*a, e, i, o, u*).

NVR SW PRPL CW—
NVR HP T S N;
BT CN TLL Y NYHW,
D RTHR S THN B N.

_____

_____

_____

_____

Instructions: Put a one-letter word on the top of the baseball pyramid; a two-letter word next, etc. Use only the letters *A,E,M,R,S,S,T.* For each successive word you must use all the letters (in any order) from the previous word and add one letter. There are several solutions.

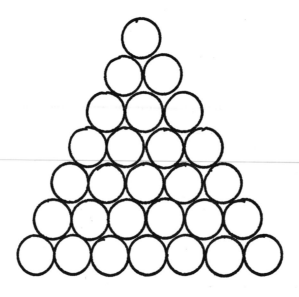

USING THE MACRON AND BREVE

Name _____ **Date** _____

Purpose: To introduce two common diacritical marks used in the dictionary as an aid to pronunciation—macron and breve. (The schwa will be explained separately.)

There once were a macron, a schwa, and a breve.
The macron was long like a slide and a sleeve,
But the breve made the letter
Sound short as in *better.*
The schwa just said, "Uh, uh, uh, uh, uh," I believe.

The macron (pronounced may′kron) is the long mark over a vowel. Example: māy
The breve (rhymes with leave) is the short mark over a vowel. Example: căt

Instructions: In the first column list ten words the dictionary would indicate with macrons (long vowel sounds). In the second column, list ten words the dictionary would indicate with breves (short vowel sounds). Mark your vowels with the appropriate marks (either a macron or breve).

When finished, check the dictionary to see how many you got right. Try for 100% on the macron and breve.

WORDS WITH MACRONS

1. _____
2. _____
3. _____
4. _____
5. _____
6. _____
7. _____
8. _____
9. _____
10. _____

WORDS WITH BREVES

1. _____
2. _____
3. _____
4. _____
5. _____
6. _____
7. _____
8. _____
9. _____
10. _____

Focus   ***USING THE SCHWA***

Name _____   **Date**_____

Purpose: To learn about the schwa sound.

Instructions: Look at the following poem for a clue to the sound of the schwa.

There once were a macron, a schwa, and a breve.
The macron was long like a slide and a sleeve,
But the breve made the letter
Sound short as in *better*.
The schwa just said, "Uh, uh, uh, uh, uh," I believe.

Fill in the missing letters which would be indicated by a schwa (upside-down *e*) in the dictionary to show the "uh" sound. You can get clues of which vowels would be correct by the related words given.

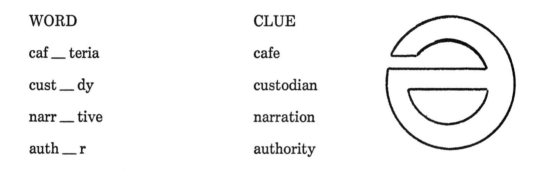

WORD	CLUE
caf __ teria	cafe
cust __ dy	custodian
narr __ tive	narration
auth __ r	authority

Now think up ten words you'd *guess* would have a schwa mark in the dictionary to show pronunciation. When you finish, consult the dictionary, and see how many you guessed correctly. Eight out of ten right shows you basically understand the schwa. More than that is GREAT!

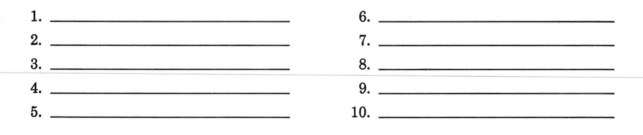

1. _____   6. _____
2. _____   7. _____
3. _____   8. _____
4. _____   9. _____
5. _____   10. _____

JOKER   **DICTIONARY JOKE**

Question: Does Friday ever come before Thursday?
Answer: Yes, in the dictionary!

JOKER   **DICTIONARY RACE**

Purpose: To see how fast students can look up information in the dictionary; to have fun using dictionaries; to deduce from this experience the main reasons for using a dictionary.

Divide the class into pairs. Let students choose their own partners. (This takes individual pressure off slower students.) Supply each pair with an identical dictionary.

Ask oral questions, and have everyone look up the answers as quickly as they can. Pick questions most students cannot figure out without using the dictionary. The object is not to test knowledge, but to practice using the dictionary with speed and accuracy.

Score one point for the first pair to answer the question correctly. (Each pair has renewed hope of being the first to get the next question!) Gear questions to the ability level of the group. Typical questions and their answers follow:

1. How do you PRONOUNCE this word? (Warning: Put unfamiliar word on board without saying it!) *efficacious* (ef-i-cā′-shus)
2. What PART OF SPEECH is *nineteen*? (noun)
3. What is a SYNONYM for *sheer*? (simple; pure; absolute; etc.)
4. How many different ENTRIES are included for *brief*?(depends on dictionary; usually at least three)
5. How many MEANINGS are given for *regulation*? (depends on dictionary; usually at least three)
6. What does *sh* ABBREVIATE? (share)
7. How many SYLLABLES does this word have? (Warning: Put word on board without saying it!) *intervocalic* (five)
8. What does *einsteinium* MEAN? (artificially produced radioactive element)
9. How many PRONUNCIATIONS are listed for *nutmeg*? (two)
10. (Warning: Be sure their dictionaries list foreign phrases before asking this.) What does the FOREIGN PHRASE, *autres temps* mean? (other times)
11. How do you spell the ADVERBIAL FORM of *admirable*? (admirably)
12. What is the PLURAL of *Ottawa*? (Ottawa or Ottawas)
13. (Warning: Be sure their dictionaries have populations listed in their supplementary sections before asking this.) What is the POPULATION of Libya? (approximately 3 million)
14. What is the ORIGIN of *prince*? (Middle English from Old French from Latin *primus* meaning "first," plus *capere* meaning "to take.")

After this exercise, deduce with them the main ways you use a dictionary:

to find meanings (definitions)
to find spellings
to find pronunciations
to find etymologies (origins)
to find correct usage
to find irregular singular and plural forms
to find parts of speech
to find general information
to find foreign words
to find syllabification
to find abbreviations

INTRO   ETYMOLOGIES

Purpose: To pique curiosity about word origins; to introduce the vocabulary word, *etymology.*

Explain two interesting word origins. The word *boycott* came from the name of a man, Captain Boycott, who was shunned and excluded by his neighbors because of political differences in Ireland in 1880. Now if you refuse to deal with someone or a company, it is called a boycott.

The word *curfew* began because of a Middle Ages law that required everyone to cover their fires at a certain hour at night. It was called "couvre-feu" meaning cover fire. They rang a bell at the couvre-feu hour. Thus our curfew, having to get off the streets at a certain hour, came about.

Give students *interesting* words to look up. Etymologies are listed in *INTERESTING ETYMOLOGIES* so you can reproduce a copy of the answers for yourself if you wish. Words should not be given in alphabetical order so students have more practice flipping through the dictionary using the alphabet and guide words. For student worksheet see *WHERE DID THE WORDS COME FROM?*

Purpose: To provide background information for teacher for use with student worksheet, *WHERE DID THE WORDS COME FROM?*

Bedlam came from Middle English *Bedlem, Bethlem,* variation of Bethlehem, an old insane asylum. St. Mary's of Bethlehem was its name. Now it is any place of noise and confusion.

Lunatic came from the Middle English *lunatik* from Old French *lunatique* from Late Latin *lunaticus* which meant moon-struck or crazy. This came from earlier Latin *luna* = moon. *Now it means anyone who is crazy.*

Calico came from Calicut, India, where the cloth was first obtained. Now it refers to certain printed cloth or spotted cats.

Sandwich was named after John Montagu, the fourth Earl of Sandwich. He ate sandwich-type food so he didn't have to leave the gambling tables to get his meals. Sandwich is a small town in England. Of course, everyone knows what a sandwich is now.

Bonfire came from bone fires used to bury the dead. In Middle English *bon* = bone and *fyr* = fire. Today it is any large outdoor fire.

School comes from Middle English *scole* from Old English *scol* from Latin *schola* = school from Greek *schole* = leisure.

Dachshund comes from German *dachs* = badger plus *hund* = dog. It still refers to a German breed of dog.

September comes from Middle English and Old French *Septembre* = 7th month of the ancient Roman year. (They began their calendar year with March.)

Hockey came from Early modern English from Old French *hoquet* = bent stick or crook from Middle Dutch *hoec* = hook. Now it is a game played with a crooked stick.

Soccer was taken from the middle letters of AS(SOC)IATION FOOTBALL.

Saxophone was named after A. J. Sax, an inventor from Belgium.

Sinister came from Middle English *sinistre* from Latin *sinister* = left hand or unlucky. In some countries, however, the left side was considered lucky.

Octopus comes from Greek *oktopous* = eight-footed from *okto* = eight plus *pous (podus)* = foot.

Focus   ***WHERE DID THE WORDS COME FROM?***

Name _____ **Date** _____

Purpose: To satisfy curiosity about word origins; to give practice in using the dictionary; to instill the concept of etymology.

Instructions: Write the etymology and definition of each word on the lines next to the word. Find:

   (1) the languages the word came from (if told)
   (2) what the foreign words meant (if told)
   (3) the person or circumstances surrounding the original word (if told)
   (4) the present definition

   1. BEDLAM_____

_____

_____

   2. LUNATIC_____

_____

_____

   3. CALICO _____

_____

_____

   4. SANDWICH_____

_____

_____

   5. BONFIRE_____

_____

_____

6. SCHOOL _____

_____

_____

7. DACHSHUND _____

_____

_____

8. SEPTEMBER _____

_____

_____

9. HOCKEY _____

_____

_____

10. SOCCER _____

_____

_____

11. SAXOPHONE _____

_____

_____

12. SINISTER _____

_____

_____

13. OCTOPUS _____

_____

_____

_____

Focus   ***BASIC SENTENCE PATTERNS***

Name_____ Date_____

Purpose: To give instruction in basic sentence patterns (common subject/predicate/ direct object or predicate nominative combinations); to present a "picture" of a sentence (diagram).

Instructions: Following are basic sentence patterns. Make diagrams and put skeleton sentences on each.

1. subject/verb

2. subject/two verbs with a joining word in between

3. two subjects with a joining word/one verb

4. two subjects with a joining word/two verbs with a joining word

5. subject/verb/direct object

6. subject/verb/predicate adjective or predicate noun

HINTS: These are what your six patterns will look like. You will have to unscramble the order!

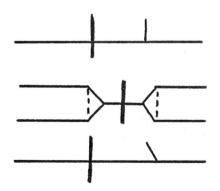
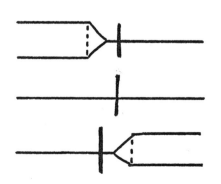

INTRO   SUBJECT/VERB RIDDLE

Purpose: To gain attention before a lesson on subject/verb agreement or verbs.

Try this oldie, but goodie:

Is it better to say, "The yolk of an egg *is* white," or, "The yolk of an egg *are* white."

(Wait for answers. Some will get this, usually.)

Answer: Neither. The yolk of an egg is YELLOW.

INTRO   WHAT'S THE OBJECT?

Purpose: To introduce the concept of direct objects in a personal and unforgettable way.

Begin the lesson by dropping your textbook loudly on the floor. This startles them to attention. Say, "I dropped my book! What is the subject of that sentence?" A bright light will respond *I*. Say, "Yes, and the ACTION verb?" They will tell you *dropped*.

Continue, "What is the direct object of the dropping?" There is not much left, but *book*. Review by stating, "*I* am the subject; *dropped* is the action I took; *book* is the object of that action."

Explain that only action verbs can have direct objects. Then involve someone in the class in your next example. Walk over to a student, hand him a long piece of chalk, and ask him to break it in half. Say, "John (name the student) broke the chalk!"

Again, go through the pattern of questions you asked earlier when you dropped the book. What is the subject? What is the action verb? Who or what is the object of the action? This absolutely captures their attention and cements the concept of direct object in the minds of the class! Continue with any lesson on direct objects.

INTRO   HOW DO YOU FEEL ABOUT HARRY?

Purpose: To introduce adjectives.

Instructions to students: Write two sentences about Harry. In the first sentence, describe Harry as if you do not like him, using descriptive words to point out how bad he looks, his negative traits, and irritating faults. In the second sentence describe Harry as if you like him very much, using descriptive words to point out how good he looks and his admirable qualities. (If your class includes a student named Harry, substitute another name.)

After the students have finished writing their sentences, call on them to read them aloud. They can choose whether to read the complimentary or insulting one. (Most will choose the latter!)

Elicit from students which words are their describing words. Perhaps put them on the chalkboard. Determine together on the basis of the definition of an adjective (a word that describes a noun or pronoun) which words are adjectives. Point out why any words they mistake for adjectives are not called adjectives.

For example, students may rightfully say adverbs are describing words. Explain that both parts of speech that describe or ADD something to the meaning of other words begin with *ad*. Do not confuse students by going deeply into adverbs at this time. Only point out (if it comes up through their errors in finding adjectives) that a describing word is called an adjective or adverb depending on what it describes. Adjectives, you repeat, describe nouns or pronouns. Then continue with other sentences the students have made up, pulling discussion from the class on which words are adjectives and deciding together why.

INTRO   BLANK THE BUILDING

Purpose: To introduce prepositions.

Write the following sentence on the chalkboard, leaving a blank where the prepositions should go. Write the sentence near the center of the chalkboard so you can make a vertical listing above, in line with, and below the sentence.

The animals went   the building.

Ask students to see how many different words fit into this sentence and make sense. (The word can make *silly* sense as long as it is grammatically correct.) Have them raise hands if they can think of a fitting word. Call on volunteers to come to the board to write their word in the blank (and above and below the blank).

Do not erase their suggestions, but keep all the prepositions up on the board at once. If anyone suggests a word that is not a preposition, leave it up until your discussion. After discussing why it doesn't apply, erase it.

Emphasize that the preposition is PRE-POSITIONED (usually comes before) its object (in this case, *building*). Point out that each preposition needs to have an object, and that the whole phrase (the preposition and its object) is called a prepositional phrase. In this example the prepositional phrase describes the verb, *went*.

Possibilities that students may suggest (or you might throw in to get them started): into, around, aboard, about, above, across, after, along, at, behind, below, beneath, beside, beyond, by, in, into, off, on, over, past, through, throughout, to, toward, under, underneath, up, upon, within.

The idea of PRE-POSITION works well in explaining a rather hard-to-explain part of speech. Also, seeing the range of prepositions at one time helps to fix the concept in their minds. Be sure they do not spell preposition incorrectly, though!

Follow this introduction with *PRE-POSITION THE PREPOSITION*. This time they will write the prepositions on their papers.

INTRO   INTERJECT YOUR EMOTION

Purpose: To introduce interjections.

Call on students, asking them to reply orally with a one- or two-word exclamation to these situational questions:

1. You just received the best birthday present you ever saw in your life. What would you say (in one word with feeling)?

2. Your friend just came rushing in to tell you about the space shuttle explosion. What would you say?

3. You just discovered an answer to a problem you have been working on for two hours. What would you say?

4. You just burned your finger on a hot stove. What would you say?

5. You just spilled your milk all over your lap. What would you say?

6. You just witnessed the winning basket for your team at a close-scoring basketball game. What would you say?

Explain that all these words are interjections. They are INTERJECTED into the sentence (thrown in, extra) to show strong feeling and emotion.

With older students you occasionally get a slang or inappropriately vulgar response. Point out (without repeating their response) that their example is definitely an interjection, but you want them to respond with appropriate language for the classroom.

Possible student interjection responses: (1) Wow! Right on! Thanks! Great! (2) Oh, no! Goodness! Bummer! (3) Aha! Finally! (4) Ouch! Ow! (5) Oops! Nuts! Whoops! (6) Yea! All right!

Focus   ***PRE-POSITION THE PREPOSITION***

Name _____   **Date**_____

Purpose: To introduce prepositions.

Instructions: Think of as many prepositions as you can that will make some sort of sense by pre-positioning them before their objects. Your teacher will tell you whether you can use your textbook list of prepositions!

1. The plane flew   the clouds.

2. The students   the seats were eating pizza.

3. The dog romped   the bus.

INTRO   DING-A-LING

Purpose: To introduce articles; to have fun with grammar.

Provide a student with a hand bell. While reading several sentences aloud, have student ring bell every time you come to a, *an,* or *the.* Tell them these are articles (also called adjectives) and the bell signals a noun is coming. As soon as one student rings bell he passes it to the next student. They enjoy this, and the bell develops conditioned responses. They soon learn to quickly identify articles and to know a noun will follow shortly.

INTRO   SUPER ACTION MAN

Purpose: To introduce action verbs.

Draw a stick man on the chalkboard with arms flailing and legs in an active position. Label him Super Action Man. Say he is very special and can do any actions that a man, monster, or animal can do. Ask what actions he could perform and list answers on board.

You will usually get physical actions first like walk or talk. If no one mentions mental actions like think, love, and understand, point out these are actions, too. Include hoot, meow, bark, and accept weird or crazy verbs, as long as they are action verbs. Remember, he is Super Action Man!

When you have a sizable number of actions (mental, physical, human, and animal), indicate they are all action verbs. Leave the drawing and examples on board during your follow-up assignment. See *ACTION MAN CAN*.

INTRO   ADVERB INTRODUCTION

Purpose: To introduce adverbs; to show the difference between an adverb and an adjective in a concrete or humorous way.

Physically show the difference in use between adverbs and adjectives by showing the difference in meaning.

Example: I smelled well. (Physically sniff around the room showing how well you carried out your smelling action.) Explain that *well* is an adverb telling how I *smelled.*

I smelled good. (Explain that because I was wearing perfume, I smelled good.) *Good* is an adjective describing *I,* the person, not describing the action of smelling or sniffing.

Example: I appeared suddenly. (Hide behind a desk, door, or somewhere. Appear suddenly.) Point out that *suddenly* is an adverb describing the action of appearing (how I appeared). *Suddenly* does not describe the person, I; I am not a "suddenly" person.

I appeared ill. Point out that *ill* describes *I,* not the action of appearing. It is *I* that is ill, not *appearing* that is ill.

Ask for a volunteer who won't be embarrassed to demonstrate for you. Then

Name_____ **Date**_____

Purpose: To practice finding action verbs.

Instructions: Circle the actions verbs. Remember, anything SUPER ACTION MAN can do is an action verb (and he can do any physical or mental action a human, animal, or monster can do!)

HANDSOME BREAK QUICKLY BARK WAS INTO

ON SEE DANCE

AN ARE AM COMPUTE

RUN JUMP MERRILY

MOO

THINK HISS

HE PLAY

HIM IS LOOK DREAM A

COMPUTER GROWL PRETTY EVERYBODY ALAS

SEEM

SHOUT

ask him to walk slowly. Point out *slowly* describes how John (insert name of actual student) is walking. It is an adverb because it is describing the action.

Then have him walk quickly. Ask someone in the class what part of speech *quickly* is and when he answers, ask why it is an adverb.

Continue, "What if I said *John is quickly*? Does that sound correct?" (They will see that it does not sound right and say so.) "What should I say, instead?" (They will say *John is quick,* or a class clown may say, *John is slow.*) Either way, you can point out that *quick* and *slow* describe John, not the action of walking.

This routine may sound long, but it only takes a few minutes. It does more to show students the difference between adjectives and adverbs than several pages of textbook practice because they (and you) are personally, kinesthetically involved.

INTRO   MISSING PARTS

Purpose: To introduce the importance of the parts of speech.
2
Make eight large cards with the name of one part of speech on each. They must be large enough to see from all seats in the room. (Students who finish assignments early can make these for you.)

Place seven cards on the chalk tray, leaving one essential card out. See if students can guess which part is missing. When they figure it out, write a sentence on the board with that part missing. (The verb is a good one to start with.) Have students supply a verb so the sentence makes sense. *Example: Jack to the store.*

Rearrange the cards and remove a different part of speech. (An adjective is a good one; nouns are too easy.) Ask them to identify the missing part. Then put a quick sentence on the board with an adjective missing, and have students supply the missing part to complete the sentence. *Example:* The dog was.

This gimmick should be used only to introduce the important role each part of speech plays. It is not designed to be a prolonged procedure or game.

JOKER   NOUN BALL

Purpose: To review and have fun with nouns.

Toss a golf whiffle ball or balloon (small, light, harmless) to any student to begin the game. The student with the ball is "it," says a word quickly, and tosses the ball to another student. The second student has to tell if the word can be used as a noun or not. If he is correct, he is "it." If he is incorrect, the first person says a new word and tosses the ball to someone else, who tells if the word can be a noun. A student can challenge another to give an example of a sentence using the word as a noun. If the student can't come up with a satisfactory response, he cannot take his turn as "it."

If the person who is "it" makes a mistake by saying the responder is wrong when he isn't (or right when he isn't), he ceases to be "it." YOU toss the ball to a person who hasn't had a chance yet, and the game continues. This gives you the opportunity to include less popular players.

This simple game does wonders for improving the quickness of decision-making on nouns. Students try to trick their friends by saying obscure or questionable nouns. You do not enter the game except as a final judge in case of disputes.

Kids enjoy the ball-tossing or balloon-bopping and have to keep alert because they never know when the object is coming their way. Limiting the ball-toss to underhand tosses is best for two reasons. First, the ball seldom goes exactly where expected because it is very light and uncontrollable. Second, there is no chance of injury from the missile of a strong-armed, enthusiastic student.

Variation: Other parts of speech can be used as students become more proficient in grammar.

JOKER   GRAMMAR UP

Purpose: To have fun while practicing parts of speech; to use as a review after studying parts of speech.

GRAMMAR UP is like a spelldown in reverse. Students follow practice sentences in their textbook naming in turn the parts of speech for each word as it comes in the sentence. You act as the judge, saying "Good," if it is right and "Up," if it is wrong. The student who misses has to stand up, but he gets a chance to sit again when his next turn comes (if he answers correctly).

Whenever anyone answers incorrectly, the other students standing at that time have a chance to answer correctly and sit down. The fairest way is to go up and down the rows (or around the tables) in the same order each time. This way all students get continuous practice, even those who have "missed" when it was their turn.

Variation: Choose teams, still using the seated positions, and proceed in the same way. The team with fewest standing at the end of the time period wins. Students really get into this game!

Variation: Let one of your better grammarians act as the judge of correctness. If you use this method, it is advisable to have a back-up judge he can confer with in case of toughies.

JOKER   CONJUNCTION JUNCTION

Purpose: To focus attention on conjunctions; to help students remember the word *conjunction* and what it means; to liken conjunctions to junctions.

By the time you get to conjunctions in the grammar hierarchy, a few students may be beginning to get the parts of speech they have already learned confused with each other. Words like conjunction and interjection start to blur in their minds because they are similar in sound and not used often enough to become a permanent part of their vocabulary.

This idea is useful after you have introduced conjunctions, but before students are able to recognize them with ease. It involves students directly and visually reinforces their learning.

On the bulletin board place two long, narrow colored strips of construction paper resembling two roads crossing (like a giant cross lying on its side with the junction in the middle). Letter the horizontal road "CONJUNCTION" and the vertical road "JUNCTION." The *N* can serve as the actual junction.

Explain that a conjunction JOINS words or parts of sentences together just like a JUNCTION joins two roads together. Pass out felt pens and a half page of construction paper (cut lengthwise and of different colors) to each student. Have them neatly print a conjunction on their paper (spelled correctly, of course!) and staple or thumbtack it to the bulletin board. The conjunctions look best mounted at various angles (even upside down in a case or two).

Have extra paper ready in case someone uses the conjunction they were thinking of. In case of duplicates, the first one to put their word up gets to keep it there. This exercise produces a bulletin board reminder that all these conjunctions are joining words. *Hint:* Do not try to use a similar tactic for each part of speech as students become confused instead of enlightened. For conjunctions, however, it will instill the concept and refresh their memories of specific words that can be used as joining words.

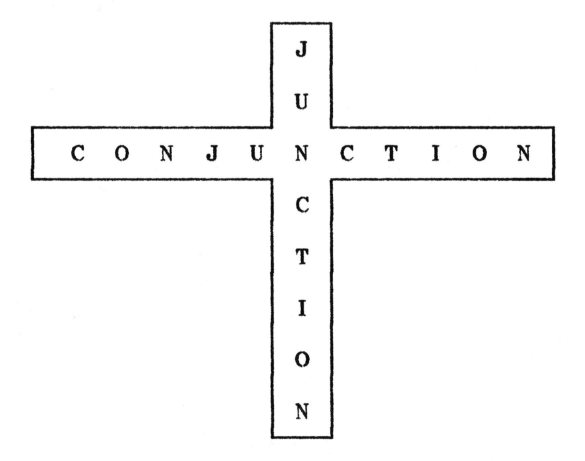

Joker   ***PRO-CROSS***

Name_____ **Date**_____

Purpose: To review personal pronouns after they have been studied in depth.

Instructions: Without using your textbook, try to work the PRO-CROSS puzzle by filling in the correct pronouns

ACROSS   *DOWN*

ACROSS

2. 3rd person singular neuter objective

5. 3rd person plural subjective

7. 3rd person singular masculine objective

8. 1st person plural objective

10. 1st person singular objective

11. 1st person singular subjective

12. 1st person plural subjective

13. 3rd person singular feminine objective

DOWN

1. 2nd person plural objective

2. 3rd person singular neuter subjective

3. 3rd person plural objective

4. 2nd person singular subjective

6. 2nd person singular objective

7. 3rd person singular masculine subjective

9. 3rd person singular feminine subjective

Focus   *PLAIN JANE*

Name_____ Date _____

Purpose: To illustrate the use of adverbs, adjectives, and verbs in making sentences more descriptive; to see where adverbs and adjectives are normally placed in sentences.

Instructions: Using each "Plain Jane" sentence as a basis, form a new, more descriptive and interesting sentence. Try a more vibrant verb and the addition of adjectives and adverbs.

Example: (Plain Jane) The girl went to the store.
              (Improved) The lazy girl sauntered slowly to the store.

1. The man walked in the woods.

_____

2. The boys were playing football.

_____

3. The principal came into the room.

_____

4. The girls worked on the computer.

_____

5. It started to rain, and the children went inside the tent.

_____

6. The students reacted to seeing the bears.

_____

7. As soon as Marlo finished, she was able to watch TV.

_____

8. Shawn won the game.

_____

9. The students read books.

_____

10. My parents ate the food in the school cafeteria.

_____

(Just for fun write your own Plain Jane and an improved version below.)

PLAIN JANE _____

IMPROVED _____

Joker   ***SOUND-ALIKES***

Purpose: To practice homonyms.

Instructions to teacher: Make a copy of these sentences for yourself and dictate sentences to students, having them orally spell the underlined word. This idea should be used after studying commonly confused homonyms. If the student you call upon spells a word incorrectly, put the confused word on the board and discuss it right then.

The key to this lesson's success is to use the names of pupils in the class and items common to their frames of reference. They listen carefully to see who you will name next and smile as they are included. Words in parentheses indicate words you should personalize. Italicized words are the homonyms being practiced. You may wish to repeat the homonym at the end of the sentence to be sure students understand which word to spell.

Variation: Have students spell homonyms on their papers.

1. (John) and (Jill) gave *their* lunches to (Robert).

2. (Carrie), will you *accept* the prize for best writing?

3. "Give me a *break!*" (Mary) shouted to (Tim).

4. (Betty) met (Thomas) at the *altar.* (This always brings a few giggles.)

5. (Jerry) forgot to put a *capital* letter in his name.

6. Language Arts is the most interesting *course* you take. (They may groan or respond in some way on this one!)

7. I want to *compliment* you on your progress.

8. Do you think I should send (Ryan) to the *counselor?*

9. Our school lunch program is serving chocolate sundaes for *dessert* today.

10. Can you *hear* me O.K.?

11. *It's* a (beautiful, rainy, or whatever is appropriate) day today.

12. (Terry) *passed* all his classes last year.

13. Friday (Avery) is going to take a *plane* out of (Detroit, New York, or whatever is nearby).

14. (Jackie), go to to the office of the *principal!* (That'll wake up any sleepy ones!)

15. I'd like to move the bulletin board, but it's *stationary.*

16. Put your books over *there* while we finish this lesson. (A few may pretend they are going to carry out your command.)

17. We're (beginning, ending, in the middle of) this *week.*

18. *Who's* going to get these all right? (Some may raise hands.)

19. *You're* sure, now, (Randy)?

20. Well, class, we're all *through* with our practice, now. (Again, you may get a happy response, but they really have had more fun than using a textbook for impersonal sentences.)

Joker   ***DOUBLE TROUBLE***

Name _____   Date_____

Purpose: To explore word and letter idiosyncracies.

ZZ   XX   EE   TT

     LL   WW   AA

      UU   SS   II

Words with Double Letters

Figure out three words for each letter below that contain the letter doubled. Example: le*tt*er.

(Don't use *that* one, now!)

(Easy Ones)   T, S, L, E

1._____   1._____   1._____   1._____

2._____   2._____   2._____   2._____

3._____   3._____   3._____   3._____

Figure out one word for each letter below that contains the letter doubled.

(Challengers)   A, W, K, I, U, Z

1. _____   4. _____

2. _____   5. _____

3. _____   6. _____

Riddle: What word contains all 26 letters? _____

Oddball Word: Most American dictionaries list only one English word beginning with

q that is not followed by a *u*. Can you find it and write it here? _____

Joker   *ALPHABET SOUP*

Name_____ Date_____

Purpose: To encourage thought about words and letters; to develop deductive reasoning skills.

Instructions: Answer each question with either one or two letters. Put your answers on the blanks provided.

_____What letter is a drink?

_____What letters are we?

_____What letter is a line?

_____What letter is an ocean?

_____What letter is an exclamation?

_____What letter is an insect?

_____What letter is a vegetable?

_____What letters describe a slippery road?

_____What letters transport blood?

_____What letter is an animal?

_____What letter is a question?

_____What letter is one of our senses?

_____What letter directs a horse?

_____What letter is a bird?

_____What letter is a verb?

_____What letter is an elevated train?

_____What letter occurs twice in a moment and not in a hundred years?

_____What letters stand for intelligence?

_____What letters are a girl's name?

_____What letters describe raspberries?

Joker   ***WORDS WITHIN WORDS***

Name_____ Date_____

Purpose: To have fun figuring out words within words.

Instructions: Find the answer to the question by using the italicized word as part of your answer.

1. What *ant* is a very, very big person?   _____

2. What *pig* is a very, very small person?   _____

3. What *bull* is shot a lot?   _____

4. What *pine* has sharp needles?   _____

5. What *pet* makes loud music?   _____

6. What *horse* grows under the ground?   _____

7. What *ox* do you need to live?   _____

8. What *cat* can propel a heavy object?   _____

9. What *cat* has pictures in it?   _____

10. What *cow* has no courage?   _____

11. What *pup* has strings?   _____

12. What *goat* is on a man's chin?   _____

13. What *cat* is found in a tree?   _____

14. What *dog* is found in a tree?   _____

15. What *bug* is in a musical instrument?   _____

16. What *kit* can fly?   _____

See if you can make up some original words within words!

_____

_____

_____

Joker   *RIDDLE FUN*

Name _____   Date _____

Purpose: To develop thinking skills; to have fun with words.

Instructions: Try to answer as many as you can.

1. What bush doesn't tell the truth?   _____

2. What bush was a politician?   _____

3. What flowers are on your face?   _____

4. What flower is a little daffy?   _____

5. What bird is a little daffy?   _____

6. What bird has a religious title?   _____

7. What bird can lift a heavy load?   _____

8. What tree is in your hand?   _____

9. What tree is two?   _____

10. What tree can compute?   _____

11. What tree is grouchy?   _____

12. What tree is a color?   _____

13. What tree can fly?   _____

14. What nut has a hole in it?   _____

15. What nut needs a bathing suit?   _____

16. What nut can you hang a picture on?   _____

17. What nut is a vegetable?   _____

18. What nut is a lady?   _____

19. What nut sounds like a sneeze?   _____

20. What nut is a country?   _____

Can you make up a word riddle? If you can, write it below.

_____

_____

INTRO   PALINDROME PALS

Purpose: To introduce any word work; to focus attention on words, the ways they are formed, and their idiosyncrasies; to introduce the term, *palindrome.*

A palindrome is a word, phrase, or sentence that is spelled the same forward or backward. They are fun to look at, think about, and make up.

Put this famous palindrome on the board: Madam, I'm Adam. Tell them if they can make up an original sentence that reads the same backward and forward, they are very clever, indeed!

Put these words on the board, and point out they are spelled the same backward or forward:

redder, deified, radar, shahs, reviver, rotator, repaper

Instructions to students: There are many shorter palindromes with two to five letters. Think of as many palindromes as you can. Ten is a good score.

Some possibilities: pep, refer, civic, sexes, madam, kayak, stats, bob, mum, nun, level, sagas, tenet, minim, noon, deed, solos, wow, did, dad, mom, peep, toot, gag, pap, tat, pop, kook, noon, bib, gig, pip, dud, poop, sis, pup, bub, boob, huh, mum.

JOKER   PLURAL PICS

Purpose: To add interest to a quiz on plurals.

Have volunteers (during free time or when finished with assignments) go through magazines and cut out pictures of animals, objects, and people. Give them a list of what to look for. The pictures can show one or more than one object. After they gather the pictures, you (or they) mount them on tagboard. Be certain the pics are large enough to be seen by students while seated. If more than one picture is on the poster board, you can number them for identification purposes.

Pictures of the following items serve as suitable quiz material: ox or oxen; man or men; woman or women; deer; silo or silos; child or children; mouse or mice; foot or feet; tooth or teeth; piano or pianos; monkey or monkeys; baby or babies; tomato or tomatoes; toy or toys; knife or knives; wolf or wolves; fox or foxes; box or boxes; potato or potatoes; puppy or puppies. They cover the basic rules for forming plurals of nouns.

Instructions to students: Number your paper from one to twenty. Write the PLURAL of the objects in each picture. Correct spelling is essential.

JOKER   PRONUNCIATION FUN

Purpose: To have fun while learning to pronounce commonly mispronounced words.

Put a tic-tac-toe form on the chalkboard. Print words on separate index cards, and stack them in a deck (face down) at the front of the room. Divide the room into two teams.

A student from Team I comes up, takes the top card, shows it to the class, and tries to pronounce the word correctly. If he is correct, he scores an *X* on the tic-tac-toe form. Then a student from Team II comes up, takes the next card, displays it, and tries to pronounce the word correctly. If he is correct, he scores an *O* on the tic-tac-toe form.

Students who are incorrect do not get to mark on the board. All students put the card on the bottom of the deck after answering. When the team makes a horizontal, vertical, or diagonal tic-tac-toe, that team wins the game.

This activity holds student interest through several games, and you can repeat it as requested throughout the year to reinforce proper pronunciation. When students obviously know the words and never miss, you can make different cards for the deck. Keep troublesome words in the deck for further practice, and retain some favorites to help with confidence. This game also helps reinforce proper spelling.

Add your own to these commonly mispronounced words: accidentally, arithmetic, athlete, athletics, calvary, candidate, cavalry, counselor, dessert, drawer, February, formerly, government, history, interesting, introduce, laboratory, library, literature, loose, lose, Massachusetts, mathematics, nuclear, particular, perform, perspire, probably, pronunciation, prostate, prostrate, quantity, recognize, sophomore, strictly, surprise.

INTRO   **PUNCTUATION RIDDLE**

Purpose: To introduce a lesson on punctuation.

Riddle: What punctuation would you use in, "I just saw a hundred-dollar bill in the hallway"?
(Wait for responses.)
Answer: Just make a dash after it!

JOKER   CLASSIC PUNCTUATION PUZZLE

Purpose: To give better students a fun challenge.

Punctuate the following classic sentences: That that is is that that is not is not that that is is not that that is not that that is not is not that that is is not that that that is

Answer: That that is, is. That that is not, is not. That that is is not that that is not. That that is not is not that that is. Is not that that? That is!

INTRO   I NEED A COMMA!

Purpose: To show how easy it is to misread sentences which have their commas omitted; to show importance of just one comma.

Put these sentences on a transparency for the overhead projector. Expose the first few words of the sentence slowly from left to right, asking students to read the sentence orally. You can, in fact, trick them with judicious use of the exposure. Uncover the words coming before the slanted line first. Substitute names of class members for Maria and Randy.

1. After washing the girls/ put on their new dresses.
2. Before starting to eat the dog/ growled loudly.
3. Before she dropped Maria/ decided to take a nap.
4. The bear must have fallen for Randy/ stopped suddenly.
(Save number four for the big finish!)

JOKER   PHONETIC PUNCTUATION

Purpose: To stimulate interest in punctuation by hearing it; to have fun with punctuation.

If you can obtain Victor Borge's recording on phonetic punctuation to play for the class, students respond well. If you can approximate his rendition yourself, they appreciate it even more! If a student becomes adept at this, let him do the reading.

With a little practice you can create sounds to represent the various punctuation marks. For example, a slight whistling sound between the teeth ending with an abrupt "ppput" with the lips (like spitting out a watermelon seed!) makes an exclamation point. You basically need only a few distinct sounds—period, comma, dash, question mark—because many can be combinations of these. (Quotation marks can be two commas; exclamation marks, a dash and period; ellipses, three periods; semi-colon, comma and a period.) Experiment until you find humorous sounds.

The following story makes an amusing one when read with sound effects representing the marks:

One day Marcia, a beautiful girl, came into the classroom. She said, "Hello, everybody! I'm glad to join you."

"Are you going to be in our class?" Tom inquired.

"No, but..."

She was interrupted by Tom who wanted to know why not—why was she not going to be a permanent member of the class?

"Alas!" she replied. "I have to do the following: get permission from the court, send for my records, and go through the enrollment process. Even then I'll be in a different class than you."

Everyone was disappointed. Oh, well... they thought... maybe we'll get a beautiful new student NEXT year!

INTRO   EXAGGERATED PUNCTUATION

Purpose: To introduce punctuation for words in a series.

While students enter the room, be writing an exaggerated series on the chalkboard. *Example:* Frank liked apples, carrots, candy, rutabagas, spinach, pears, peanuts, milk, pie, cake, and cookies. They will be curious about when you will stop and what you will say Frank likes. The name you use should be a student in class. Make it as long as your chalkboard and time permit, and include some unlikely items for attention-getting.

Ask if anyone knows the rule for the commas used in the sentence. Elicit the words in a series rule.

Then write: Jackie ran, jumped, (and have them come to the board to add others verbs for the series, being careful they put commas as required). Last, begin an unfinished sentence for them as follows: **Sam went into the barn, behind the stall....** Then have them offer suggestions for other prepositional phrases in a series to continue the sentence.

Using exaggerated examples and actual class members' names adds to the interest and fun of this introduction. Students remember the rule involving words in a series because they participated in its discovery.

FOCUS   HARD SPELL

Purpose: To challenge your better spellers.

The following ten words are considered among the most difficult to spell. Give them only to your top students who feel bored with the regular spelling words. Students should look up definitions of any words that they do not understand.

inoculate	rarefy
embarrass	vilify (vilefy)
harass	plaguing
supercede (supersede)	desiccate
innuendo	picnicking

FOCUS **SPELLING PRACTICE**

Purpose: To practice spelling new words.

Make flash cards (or have early finishers make them). Each card should be large enough to be seen from the back of the room.

Flash cards one at a time for a few moments (three seconds is about right for most groups). Instruct them to write or print the word correctly on their individual papers. There is no pressure to this practice. Students make corrections on their own papers as you spell the words correctly at the conclusion of the practice. The students then know which words they need to study at home, and have the correct spellings to use as a guide.

JOKER **SPELL REVIEW**

Purpose: To have fun practicing and reviewing spelling words.

Divide students into four teams. Balance the teams to keep the scores close. Divide the chalkboard into four sections, each numbered from one to ten.

Pronounce the word. First members of each team (four at once) go to board quickly, write word, and return to seat. A time limit adds excitement to the game. Pronounce second word, and so on.

Give a good speller the spelling list and the responsibilities of correcting the words and keeping the team scores. The words should be corrected after each ten, with one point awarded for each correct word. The scorekeeper should post the scores at the tops of each column, keeping only the running totals.

Erase words after each ten, leaving the numbers intact, and continue for a specified period of time. The team with the most points wins.

JOKER **KINESTHETIC SPELLING**

Purpose: To practice spelling with physical as well as mental involvement; to have fun while learning to spell.

This activity works best with *younger or slower* children. Tack letters on each child with a safety (not straight) pin. Call a word from their spelling list or reading list. Children go to the front of the room as fast as they can and spell it out with their bodies.

Be sure to have more than one of the most common letters, such as vowels. You will have to look over your word list and provide needed letters. *Usually* letters like Q, Z, and X can be omitted unless you know they're necessary for the specific list being studied. (Also, you don't want to saddle a student with an unpopular letter if you don't have to, as it reduces his chances of gaining points and cuts down on his participation.)

Variation: For older students pass out large cards with letters on them. (Cut-up file folders work fine.) Have the students go to the front of the room, holding up the cards of the correct letters to spell the words. If you give each student in the group one point for spelling the word within thirty seconds, you will get more enthusiastic cooperation. The student with the most points at the end of the practice wins.

JOKER   WORDLE

Purpose: To practice spelling and vocabulary.

Make several sets of alphabets (or have students make them) using felt pens and unlined index cards. By cutting each 3″ × 5″ card in half, you get two letter cards of the right size. Keep the alphabets in sets, as you may think of other uses for them.

WORDLE is a simplified form of Scrabble. When students play, each student takes seven unknown letters. He may choose letters from any of the alphabet sets, but cannot look to see what he is getting. Students lay the letters face-up on the table in front of them.

Students take turns placing a letter on the table. They try to form words by placing their letters adjacent to ones on the table in any direction. If a student is able to play more than one letter in succession to form a word during his turn, he is allowed to do so. Otherwise, he plays one letter only. Each letter played counts one point, whether or not it forms a word. (This gives less able students points because they play at least one letter each turn!)

In addition, when someone completes a word, it counts the same as the total number of letters in it. (*Table* would count five points.) Add the total letters in completed words to the points awarded for played letters during the turns to get the total point counts. The student with the most points at the end of the time allowed is the winner. This game is suitable for two to three players, and is handy for early-finishers.

JOKER   SPELLDOWN WITH A TWIST

Purpose: To practice proper spelling of words.

This is a traditional spelling bee with a twist. Ask students to count off one-two, one-two. Have all the students saying "one" stand on one side of the room; all the students saying "two" on the other. Give spelling words, first to one side, then the other, waiting for their spellings.

The twist is this. If a student misses a word, he must return to his seat, write the word correctly ten times, and hand it in to you. He may then rejoin his team! This method keeps even slower students productively occupied while "out" and continually involves every student in the learning process. Those who need the practice most get it!

INTRO   SYLLABLE RIDDLES

Purpose: To introduce lesson on syllabification.

Riddle: What word can you pronounce quicker by adding a syllable to it? (Repeat, if needed.)
(Wait for guesses.)

Answer: Quick.

Riddle: What word becomes shorter when you add a syllable to it? (They should get this one if they listened to the first one.)

Answer: Short.

INTRO   BEAT THE RHYTHM

Purpose: To introduce the syllables and accents of words; to involve students personally and kinesthetically.

Liken the syllables and accents of words to the beat or rhythm in songs. Tell them you are going to beat out a popular Christmas song to see if they can guess it. Beat out the rhythm of "Jingle Bells." See if anyone can identify it. (They usually can.)

Follow this by having them beat out their own names. Be sure Jennifer beats louder on the Jen and gets all three beats in. Let them practice a bit. Then you tap out students' names and have them raise their hands if they recognize their beats.

FOCUS   CLASSROOM SYLLABLES

Purpose: To practice syllabification and accents; to involve students personally.

Run off lists of the first and last names of all students in your class. Distribute. Ask them to make five columns on their papers, labeling them 1, 2, 3, 4, and 5. They are to classify each name by the number of syllables it has. *Example:*

1	2	3	4	5
John	Mary	Teresa	Issyono	(none)
Tom	Judy	Overton		
Joan	Jason	Jennifer		
Smith	Parker	Parkinson		
	Grabinsk	McPherson		
	Zulu			

With the same class lists, have students classify which syllable is accented in the names (first, second, third, and so on). *Example:*

1	2	3
John'	Te re'sa	Is sy on'o
Tom'	Gra binsk'	
Joan'	Mc Pher'son	

Smith'

Mar'y

Ju'dy

Ja'son

Park'er

Zu'lu

O'ver ton

Jen'ni fer

Park'in son

JOKER   FLASH CARD VOCAB

Purpose: To practice vocabulary words; to have fun with vocabulary definitions and synonyms.

Make (or have students make) flash cards of vocabulary words. On the back write the definition or synonym. Be sure to use one color for the vocabulary word and a different color for the synonym or definition. Otherwise, you may flash the wrong side of the card.

To practice, flash the synonym or definition to the class. Let them say aloud the vocabulary word together. After they get better at it, divide into teams. Go down the row or around the room in logical order, flashing one card at a time. If the student gets it right, give him the card to hold. If he gets it wrong, go on to the next student. The team holding the most cards at the end of the game is the winner. (You will need about fifty vocabulary flash cards to make this game work smoothly.) The game is over when you are out of cards.

JOKER   VOCAB BINGO

Purpose: To have fun while reviewing vocabulary words.

Collect (and ask students to collect) toothpaste caps or other objects to use as markers on their cards. (They will collect them enthusiastically if they know the purpose.) Pennies work well, also.

Divide a sheet of paper into twenty-five squared areas. Type or print vocabulary words in a different order on each card, making one card per student. You will need a teacher assistant or extra help for this, but it is well worth the trouble. Students like this game, and learn the definitions of words more quickly than by most other methods. It is a game you can play frequently throughout the year to reinforce vocabulary.

You will need a master list of vocabulary words and their synonyms. Many reading, literature, and English textbooks have such lists furnished with their materials.

To play the game, call off synonyms of words. If a student has the word on his card that matches the synonym you call, he places a marker on it. Student calls "VOCAB" when he makes an up-and-down, across, or diagonal line with five squares marked.

See *VOCAB BINGO* for blank master sheet. Put one vocabulary word in each square. Make each card different from every other card. Use a master list to make the cards systematically different from each other. Lightweight tagboard is great, but regular unlined paper can be used. If your school has a laminating machine, have the cards laminated to last longer.

Joker   ***VOCAB BINGO***

Purpose: To have fun while increasing your vocabulary.

Instructions: When you hear a synonym for one of the words on your card, place a marker on the square. When you get five squares covered, horizontally, vertically, or diagonally, declare "VOCAB!" If you can pronounce all the words back to the caller correctly, you win *VOCAB BINGO*.

V O C A B B I N G O				

Section IV

SPEAKING, LISTENING,
AND ORAL PRESENTATION

FOCUS   **CHORAL READING**

Purpose: To increase oral reading skills; to help instill cooperative teamwork and class cohesiveness.

Choral reading is oral group reading. The class acts as a choir or chorus might with various voices taking different parts. Choose a narrative poem or other interesting reading material that divides naturally into different voice ranges. Divide the class into groups and read orally in unison by male, female, or other grouping. Include solos as needed.

Poems which have several people engaged in dialogue or which have narrative and dialogue repeatedly interspersed offer the best chances for successful choral reading. Prose, too, can be used effectively.

One poem which lends itself to choral reading is "The Raven" by Edgar Allan Poe. Group I can read the first person accounts. (Girls do this nicely.) Group II can read any quotations of the man or his thoughts. (Boys do this well.) Group III can read the raven's lines with an air of mystery and slowness. (This is a good part for less capable readers since it is mostly composed of "Nevermore" and comes in rather predictably at the ends of verses.) See *THE RAVEN* for a printed copy of the full poem with parts marked.

THE RAVEN is prepared for classroom use so each student can have a copy to study before being asked to choral read. Clear up vocabulary and pronunciation problems before the group reading. See *THE RAVEN VOCAB HELPER*. Call this a rehearsal. When students are prepared ahead of time, they will read with confidence, put appropriate expression in their voices, and be able to keep their groups together as a unit while reading. Encourage short pauses at commas and semicolons, longer pauses at the ends of sentences, and practice more difficult passages before the final reading.

The poem is marked for appropriate participatory groups: (G) for girls, (B) for boys, (A) for all. Other divisions of groups do just as well, depending upon the class members and their attributes. Use "The Raven" for the fun of its interesting sound patterns, rhymes, and rhythms, rather than emphasizing its allusions or rather dark mood.

Students are hesitant at first to do choral reading but quickly learn to enjoy it. You can liken choral reading to its popular modern version, rapping, as most students are familiar with this. You may want to use *RAPPING* as an introductory fun activity before trying "The Raven" as a more serious, choral reading.

Rapping often involves slang, idioms, or street talk. It is characterized by repetitive rhythms and simple end and internal rhyme patterns. These often appeal to young people, and you can use rapping to illustrate these concepts.

Purpose: To use as choral reading (adapted from "The Raven" by Edgar Allan Poe).

Instructions: Read parts as indicated. (G) = Girls; (B) = Boys; (A) = All

(G) Once upon a midnight dreary, while I pondered, weak and weary,
Over many a quaint and curious volume of forgotten lore—
While I nodded, nearly napping, suddenly there came a tapping,
As of some one gently rapping, rapping at my chamber door.
(B) " 'Tis some visitor," I muttered, "tapping at my chamber door—
Only this and nothing more."

(G) Ah, distinctly I remember it was in the bleak December;
And each separate dying ember wrought its ghost upon the floor.
Eagerly I wished the morrow—vainly I had sought to borrow
From my books surcease of sorrow—sorrow for the lost Lenore—
For the rare and radiant maiden whom the angels name Lenore—
Nameless *here* for evermore.

(G) And the silken, sad, uncertain rustling of each purple curtain
Thrilled me—filled me with fantastic terrors never felt before;
So that now, to still the beating of my heart, I stood repeating
(B) " 'Tis some visitor entreating entrance at my chamber door—
Some late visitor entreating entrance at my chamber door;—
This it is and nothing more."

(G) Presently my soul grew stronger; hesitating then no longer,
(B) "Sir," said I, "or Madam, truly your forgiveness I implore;
But the fact is I was napping, and so gently you came rapping,
And so faintly you came tapping, tapping at my chamber door,
That I scarce was sure I heard you"—
(G) here I opened wide the door;—
(A) Darkness there and nothing more.

From Complete Stories and Poems of Edgar Allan Poe, Doubleday & Company, Inc., New York, N.Y., 1966.

(G) Deep into that darkness peering, long I stood there wondering, fearing,
Doubting, dreaming dreams no mortal ever dared to dream before;
But the silence was unbroken, and the stillness gave no token,
And the only word there spoken was the whispered word,
(B) "Lenore!"
(G) This I whispered, and an echo murmured back the word
(B) "Lenore!"
(A) Merely this and nothing more.

(G) Back into the chamber turning, all my soul within me burning,
Soon again I heard a tapping somewhat louder than before.
(B) "Surely," said I, "surely that is something at my window lattice;
Let me see, then, what thereat is, and this mystery explore—
Let my heart be still a moment and this mystery explore;—
'Tis the wind and nothing more!"

(G) Open here I flung the shutter, when, with many a flirt and flutter
In there stepped a stately Raven of the saintly days of yore.
Not the least obeisance made he; not a minute stopped or stayed he;
But, with mien of lord or lady, perched above my chamber door—
Perched upon a bust of Pallas just above my chamber door—
Perched, and sat, and nothing more.

(G) Then this ebony bird beguiling my sad fancy into smiling,
By the grave and stern decorum of the countenance it wore,
(B) "Though thy crest be shorn and shaven, thou," I said, "are sure no craven,
Ghastly grim and ancient Raven wandering from the Nightly shore—
Tell me what thy lordly name is on the Night's Plutonian shore!"

THE RAVEN (Continued)

(A) Quoth the Raven, "Nevermore."

(G) Much I marvelled this ungainly fowl to hear discourse so plainly,
Though its answer little meaning—little relevancy bore;
For we cannot help agreeing that no living human being
Ever yet was blessed with seeing bird above his chamber door—
Bird or beast upon the sculptured bust above his chamber door,
With such name as "Nevermore."

G) But the Raven, sitting lonely on the placid bust, spoke only
That one word, as if his soul in that one word he did outpour.
Nothing farther then he uttered—not a feather then he fluttered—
Till I scarcely more than muttered
(B) "Other friends have flown before—
On the morrow *he* will leave me, as my hopes have flown before."
(A) Then the bird said "Nevermore."

(G) Startled at the stillness broken by reply so aptly spoken,
(B) "Doubtless," said I, "what it utters is its only stock and store
Caught from some unhappy master whom unmerciful Disaster
Followed fast and followed faster till his songs one burden bore—
Till the dirges of his Hope that melancholy burden bore
Of 'Never—nevermore.' "

(G) But the Raven still beguiling all my fancy into smiling,
Straight I wheeled a cushioned seat in front of bird, and bust and door;
Then, upon the velvet sinking, I betook myself to linking
Fancy unto fancy, thinking what this ominous bird of yore—
What this grim, ungainly, ghastly, gaunt, and ominous bird of yore
Meant in croaking "Nevermore."

(G) This I sat engaged in guessing, but no syllable expressing
To the fowl whose fiery eyes now burned into my bosom's core;
This and more I sat divining, with my head at ease reclining
On the cushion's velvet lining that the lamp-light gloated o'er,
But whose velvet violet lining with the lamp-light gloating o'er,
She shall press, ah, nevermore!

(G) Then, methought, the air grew denser, perfumed from an unseen censer.
Swung by Seraphim whose foot-falls tinkled on the tufted floor.
(B) "Wretch," I cried, "thy God hath lent thee—by these angels he hath sent thee
Respite—respite and nepenthe from thy memories of Lenore;
Quaff, oh quaff this kind nepenthe and forget this lost Lenore!"
(A) Quoth the Raven "Nevermore."

THE RAVEN (Continued)

(B) "Prophet!" said I, "thing of evil!—prophet still, if bird or devil!—
Whether Tempter sent, or whether tempest tossed thee here ashore,
Desolate yet all undaunted, on this desert land enchanted—
On this home by Horror haunted—tell me truly, I implore—
Is there—*is* there balm in Gilead?—Tell me—tell me, I implore!"

(A) Quoth the Raven "Nevermore."

(B) "Prophet!" said I, "thing of evil!—prophet still, if bird or devil!
By that Heaven that bends above us—by that God we both adore—
Tell this soul with sorrow laden if, within the distant Aidenn,
It shall clasp a sainted maiden whom the angels name Lenore—
Clasp a rare and radiant maiden whom the angels name Lenore."

(A) Quoth the Raven "Nevermore."

(B) "Be that word our sign of parting, bird or fiend!" I shrieked, upstarting—
"Get thee back into the tempest and the Night's Plutonian shore!
Leave no black plume as a token of that lie thy soul hath spoken!
Leave my loneliness unbroken!—quit the bust above my door!"
Take thy beak from out my heart, and take thy form from off my door!"

(A) Quoth the Raven "Nevermore."

(G) And the Raven, never flitting, still is sitting, *still* is sitting
On the pallid bust of Pallas just above my chamber door;
And his eyes have all the seeming of a demon's that is dreaming,
And the lamp-light o'er him streaming throws his shadow on the floor;
And my soul from out that shadow that lies floating on the floor
Shall be lifted—nevermore!

Focus   ***THE RAVEN VOCAB HELPER***

(Vocabulary in Order of Appearance in Poem)

Purpose: To help you understand the words used in THE RAVEN so you can read it with more expression and meaning.

Instructions: Think about the meanings, and ask about any words you do not know how to pronounce.

pondered	thought; meditated
quaint	old-fashioned
lore	knowledge
chamber	room
bleak	gloomy
morrow	tomorrow
surcease	end
entreating	asking
peering	staring
token	clue
lattice	cross-piece in door/window
obeisance	respect
mien	manner
bust	statue of head and shoulders
Pallas	mythological Greek goddess
beguiling	charming
fancy	imagination
grave	serious
decorum	properness
countenance	expression
crest	tuft on top of head
craven	coward
Plutonian shore	edge of underworld
ungainly	clumsy
discourse	speech
relevancy	importance
placid	smooth; undisturbed
aptly	cleverly
dirges	death marches
melancholy	sad
ominous	threatening
gaunt	starved

yore	time long past
bosom	chest
divining	guessing
censer	incense burner
Seraphim	angel
respite	rest
nepenthe	potion to relieve pain
quaff	drink
balm	comfort
Giliad	mountainous place in Palastine
implore	beg
tempest	storm
laden	burdened
Aidenn	paradise
quit	leave

Purpose: To learn to read orally in unison.

Instructions: Rapping is a modern variation of choral reading. It involves highly rhythmic recitation of serious or humorous poetry or prose. Try this ''rap'' on for size. Try to keep together while rapping. It helps to tap your foot, snap your fingers, or use body movements to the rhythm.

(All:) Come on, gang, let's start to rap.
Let's keep the rhythm, tap, tap, tap!
We're gonna read at the very same time,
And even try to put down a rhyme.
All you girls, now, let's rehearse.
You're gonna do the very next verse.

(Girls:) You are next, boys, so don't laugh!
Try to rap without a gaff.

(Boys:) Uh-oh! You were right, of course.
Now here's a couplet in full force.

(All:) Rapping can be lots of fun.
It's really sad that we are done.

(Girls:) Maybe we can write our own,
And practice on the telephone.

(Boys:) Or better yet, we'll write some now;
We're good at it, 'cause we know how!

(All:) O.K., gang, let's stop this thing,
And see what raps our papers bring!

Instructions:
Now that everyone has the idea, write your own raps.
We'll pick several to read orally as a class.

Focus

COMMUNICATION SCRAMBLE

Purpose: To bring to mind basic elements of communication used throughout history; to enjoy solving scrambled words.

Instructions: Unscramble the following items used in communication. If you solve them all, you will have traced the history of communication from cave days until the present.

1. enthlepeo _____

2. reet lebza _____

3. retlet _____

4. gins galnegua _____

5. daroi _____

6. seroM deco _____

7. erypicshioglh _____

8. obok _____

9. vetiolnies _____

10. tedvaipoe _____

11. mekos nigals _____

12. mudr ebat _____

13. pespanwer _____

14. civoe _____

15. geleparth _____

16. zigemana _____

17. letamarg _____

18. yobd ganglaue _____

19. restueg _____

20. oemiv _____

JOKER   **DON'T REPEAT THIS, BUT . . .**

Purpose: To show how gossip and rumors get started; to see how stories can change through retelling.

Quickly whisper a short, but involved story to one student. Be sure to have lots of numbers and confusing details in it. Begin, "Don't repeat this, but . . ." Then instruct the student to whisper it to his neighbor. If you have a small class, let the story go all the way around the room. Halfway around is enough in a large class or the others will become bored while waiting for their turns.

When the gossip gets all the way around, have the last student repeat to the class what he heard. Then you tell the story you began. See how closely they resemble each other. Discuss why they are different and the relationship between truth and gossip. (Sometimes you *think* you heard something you really didn't hear; sometimes you get confused about the details even though you are trying to be truthful; some people naturally embellish stories with their imaginations.)

The following example takes about twenty seconds for the first telling. (The time usually decreases as it goes around the room, as the story tends to get shorter when students forget parts of it.) Younger or slower students should be told a shorter story; older students, a more complicated one. *Example:*

Don't repeat this, but . . . You know my cousin's husband's aunt named Marelda? Well, she was only 16-1/2 when her mother fell into the 15-foot well at her brother's farm. All the neighbors had to help get her out, and fortunately she only broke her left leg and the second toe on her right foot. Poor thing—here she was all bandaged up and on crutches when a robber came! I remember it was the 14th day of May at 7:00 o'clock in the evening. Good old Marelda! She said she was glad she had fallen because she was able to threaten him with her crutch, and he ran away, never to be seen again.

FOCUS   **PARTNER PANTOMIME**

Purpose: To develop pantomime skill; to develop cooperative planning skills; to have fun.

Divide the class into partners. (For this one it is best to let them choose their own.) Students plan together to present a fairy tale or simple story to the class. One person pantomimes the story, while the other provides the voice.

Have plenty of stories available in your room, or arrange for the librarian to set up a display of appropriate story books. Allow twenty minutes for planning (picking out the story, deciding who will read or tell the story, who will do the pantomime, and what actions will be used). The performances will usually take only a few minutes each. If you have twelve to fifteen pairs, you should be able to complete this project in an average class period.

FOCUS   **THERE'LL BE SOME CHANGES MADE**

Purpose: To develop cooperative spirit; to increase skills of observation and recall.

Instructions to students: Choose a person near you for your partner. Face each other and carefully observe each other.

Your teacher will signal you to turn away from your partner. During this time, each of you will make five changes in jewelry, hair, clothing, or whatever. After another signal from your teacher, face your partner again, and try to determine the changes. If you get all five right, you are very observant!

INTRO   **ALL TALK**

Purpose: To show (dramatically) differences in sound levels; to introduce group activity and the importance of group cooperation in keeping noise levels down.

With no previous discussion, have everyone in the class say their names at the same time. Immediately afterwards, have everyone whisper their names softly at the same time.

Students are surprised at the vast difference in noise level. Explain that each group must whisper or talk softly while planning and doing group work so that people can hear each other in their own groups and not disturb other groups. Point out that if each person talks in his normal voice, this is an example of how loud it would be. Emphasize that this level of loudness is not acceptable in the classroom.

JOKER   **ORAL STORY GAMES**

Purpose: To provide fun and stimulation; to encourage imagination and thinking skills; to build self-confidence.

Begin a story around the room. Start with *Once.* You can bet the next three words will be *upon a time!* But from there on it will get interesting. Each student adds one word until the story is completed. It will take several times around the room to complete a story. Encourage rapid responses to keep the story moving quickly and students actively involved.

Variation: One person says a word. The second repeats it and adds one more word. The third person repeats both words and adds one more. Go until no one can repeat the words in correct order. (These words do not have to form a story and can be unrelated.)

Variation: Begin, *Once upon a time there were 26 middle school students from* (name your school). Let them continue orally by calling on another student to add a sentence to the story. That student then calls on another, etc. This encourages rapid thought processes, and keeps the game interesting, as students never know who will be called upon next.

Variation: Pick an object from a pillow case, sack, or bag. Give two sentences relating to it to begin a story. The next student picks a different object and continues the same story with two more sentences relating to the new object, etc. Insist that the story makes sense, even though it is bound to be humorous.

Variation: Take turns around the room with each person saying a rhyming word. When students get stuck and rhymes run out, start a new one. Remind students of how many words in a row they were able to rhyme, and encourage them to keep trying to break their record.

Variation: Students read a story aloud. Instruct students to stop suddenly in the middle of a sentence and call on another student to continue reading. (This keeps them alert!)

FOCUS   CLASS DISCUSSION

Purpose: To learn to solve problems cooperatively; to develop skill in participating in group discussion.

Present real class problems for discussion. Set up ground rules as follows:

1. No one can dominate the discussion.
2. No one can interrupt.
3. No one can verbally attack or ridicule another person.
4. Focus on ideas and solutions to problems.
5. Majority rules (subject to veto power of teacher).
6. Everyone must participate.

Problems will vary with the class and school. Typical class discussions include the following:

1. Planning a class trip.
2. Solving a class problem.
3. Solving a school problem.
4. Planning a class party.
5. Planning the direction of class work (topics to study next).
6. Planning a group project.
7. Planning for a voluntary group service project.
8. Deciding on a guest to invite to class.
9. Dividing into groups for a special purpose.
10. How to help a seriously ill student.
11. How to help a new student.
12. How to help an unsuccessful student.

FOCUS   MINI-DEBATES

Purpose: To learn to defend opinions logically; to gain ease in speaking in front of others.

Formal debates often take too much time for use in regular language arts classes, but mini-debates work. Give each student two minutes for his presentation. See *MINI-DEBATING*.

Variation: Have students conduct panel discussions with four in a group. Each student takes one portion of the topic and presents it to the class. Two minutes per student is sufficient.

Variation: Have students conduct a round-table discussion on the topic of their choice. As many as six students per topic engage each other in an informal discussion in front of the class.

FOCUS   MAKE A DIORAMA

Purpose: To encourage creativity; to promote cooperative planning and spirit.

Have students bring in appropriate materials during the week preceding this activity.

Instructions to students: A diorama is a miniature scene, usually in three dimensions. Work in groups of three to construct a diorama using a shoe box, pipe cleaners (for people), frozen dessert sticks, empty thread spools, or any other aids you can locate. Use your imagination to come up with inexpensive items to represent the people and objects in the scene. The diorama should depict a scene from one of the plays or stories the class has read.

Variation: Design the setting without characters.

INTRO AND FOCUS   MIKE MAGIC

Purpose: To acquaint students with their own voices; to get over "mike fright"; to build confidence speaking in front of others.

Typical younger students have had little or no experience with microphone use. Talking into a mike and hearing their own voices for the first time can be a bit scary and embarrassing, but students universally enjoy it after the giggles and sweaty palms are over.

Set up a simple public address system in your classroom. For an initial experience, ask each student to introduce himself to the class, giving name, age, and one special activity he likes to do. (This is enough for the first time!) They will nervously and quickly participate, usually with grimaces, laughter, and odd facial expressions.

It is a good idea to tape-record their introductions and play the recording back to them. This way they not only hear the amplified voice in the room as they speak (which is shocking if they've never heard it before), but also their recorded voice (which sounds different than when they hear it through their own ears). (See page 199.)

Focus   ***MINI-DEBATING***

Purpose: To gain ease in speaking in front of others; to learn to defend your views logically.

Instructions: You are going to have the opportunity to express your views on a topic. Prepare yourself adequately to defend your view forcefully. You need not actually believe in the side you are defending, as long as you can put forth your ideas in a persuasive manner.

1. Get into groups of four.

2. Choose one of the topics below or submit an original topic to your teacher for approval. The topic should be stated in the affirmative.

3. Decide who will be FOR the issue and who will be AGAINST the issue. (Two students will defend each side.)

4. The first speaker will speak for the affirmative; the second for the negative; the third can try to break down the arguments of the second (negative side) speaker, plus summarize the affirmative; the last speaker can break down the arguments of the first and third speakers (affirmative side) and summarize the negative viewpoint.

5. Arm yourself with good, solid facts and logic. You may go to the library for information, if needed, but most topics will not necessitate library use.

Topic suggestions:

1. Students should be able to wear makeup before ninth grade.

2. All teachers should be called by their first names.

3. Students should be allowed to wear anything they want to school classes.

4. There should be a morning snack break for school students.

5. Students should trade places with teachers for a day.

6. Students should be required to wear school uniforms.

7. Pop and candy should be banned from the school premises.

8. All young people should have the responsibility of caring for a pet.

9. Everyone should have a brother or sister.

10. All students should be required to take English.

From this simple beginning you can work up to recording speeches, skits, and improvisations. They can record entire plays. Especially suitable are dramatic presentations that call for expressive voices and a multitude of sound effects.

After the students become comfortable in the classroom setting, try transferring them into an auditorium. Again, use the public address system with a microphone. This is a giant leap, even for those who have built confidence in the more familiar environment of the classroom.

For the auditorium debut allow them to read material of their choice. Suggest short stories, the telling of several jokes, poetry reading, or an excerpt from a longer piece of writing. They should be given class time to prepare, ask about pronunciations or meanings, and rehearse with a friend. Several days should elapse between their class rehearsal and the final auditorium reading so they can also practice at home.

JOKER   BULLETIN BOARD IDEA

Purpose: To build self-image; to emphasize uniqueness of the individual.

Put up a bulletin board calendar with birthdays of every student marked.
Variation: If you can obtain a "school picture" of each student, use the picture to mark the day instead of the name.

JOKER   THANK-YOU BOX

Purpose: To build self-image; to build social skills; to instill kindness.

Provide a box (a shoe box works fine) with "Thank-You Box" or similar title on it. Encourage students to write thank-you notes (either signed or unsigned) to their classmates or teacher. The notes should be sincere and reflect actual situations.

Write a few notes yourself to get and keep the idea rolling. Once a week you can read them to the class. It is better if you do the reading so there is no chance of recognition of penmanship. You will find many students like to admit they wrote a note, and this is fine, but you should not reveal the names. This activity has no negative side effects and helps create positive class spirit.

FOCUS   STORY TIME

Purpose: To learn how to tell or read a story to others; to practice oral reading with an expressive voice; to build self-image.

See if you can arrange to have your students tell or read stories to younger children. The young ones enjoy it, and the process helps develop confidence in the older students. If you have elementary students in your building or a nearby building, the principal can facilitate this. There should be a gap of several grades between the reader and the listener. (It is easier to read to appreciative, younger students than to one's peers.)

Focus   ***STORY TIME***

Purpose: To learn how to tell or read a story to others; to practice oral reading with an expressive voice.

Instructions: You are going to learn to read a story effectively to younger children. Follow the steps below.

1. Choose a story, two to three minutes in length, that you enjoy and can read fluently. Children especially like the following:

Fairy tales

Fables

"Off the wall" stories

Unusual stories

Scary stories

Stories with rhyme and rhythm

Stories with fun names

Folk tales

Tall tales or legends

Colorfully or unusually illustrated stories

Humorous stories

2. Check with the teacher to be sure the story is appropriate for the age level of your audience.

3. Practice the story on your own. (Parents and brothers or sisters make a great audience!) You also will be given at least one opportunity to read it to our class for practice.

4. Points to keep in mind while practicing:

Hold the book so children can see the pictures

Speak in a voice all can hear

Speak in an expressive voice

Look up from the book to make eye contact with your audience whenever you can

Change your voice for different characters

Rehearse adequately

JOKER   **STAGE FRIGHT ELIMINATOR**

Purpose: To help eliminate "stage fright"; to build self-image; to learn to express thoughts through gestures.

The time-tested game of charades livens up the class and is useful in a variety of settings. The goal is to pantomime the title of a book, story, character, or poem, and to have the audience guess the title in a specified time. You can limit the category to books only, combine several categories, or include movies, television programs, names of states, or other topics. Decide as a class what your overall topic will be. Students can make up their own individual titles to pantomime, or you can have a "hatful" ready. Students can then pull one out of the hat when they come to the front of the room.

If some class members have not played charades before, it is helpful to pass out *CHARADES* and demonstrate a simple example before they begin the game. *Example:* WASHINGTON

1st clue: 1st finger up and then a fist (one word)
2nd clue: Three fingers up and hit your wrist with flat hand (three syllables in the word)
3rd clue: 1st finger up and hit your wrist with flat hand (1st syllable)
4th clue: Pantomime washing your hands ("wash" or "washing")
5th clue: Three fingers up and hit your wrist with flat hand (3rd syllable)
6th clue: Finger to ear lobe (sounds like)
7th clue: In pantomime make a circle with your arms; then indicate you've been sweating by wiping your brow ("sun"—sounds like "ton").

You can make up your own signals or use typical ones as shown in *CHARADES*. Two minutes per charade is an appropriate time limit.

Variation: Play charades by keeping the time used as the score for the individual pantomimist. The person who uses the LEAST amount of time to get the idea across is the winner. This involves a timer and scorekeeper, and gives students an incentive to give precise clues.

Variation: If you have more time, you can play charades in teams. Whoever guesses the correct answer gets a point for that team. If no one answers in two minutes, no points are awarded, and someone from the opposite team takes a turn.

Variation: Team charades can be played with the pantomimist performing for his own team to guess the title. If his team guesses correctly within the time limit, they get a point. If they don't, the opposing team has the chance to guess and win the point. The opposing team, however, does not get additional time or clues.

To keep students from "helping" their team members by whispering the answer, it is prudent to use a "hatful" of titles you have prepared ahead of time. Have students pull the topics from the hat just before their turn.

When there is an uneven number of players, one student can keep the score on the chalkboard. This is a suitable activity for the occasional student who does not like to play charades.

Joker   ***CHARADES***

Purpose: To familiarize you with the game of charades.

Charades is a fun game where you pantomime the name of a movie, story, television program, character, poem, or other category. The audience tries to guess the title. Don't talk except to respond to let the mimic know you are guessing in the right direction.

Instructions: Think of two items to pantomime. (one extra in case someone else acts out yours before your turn). You will have up to two minutes to complete your pantomime. If no one guesses it, you will have to tell us what it represented. Whoever guesses the answer correctly does his pantomime next.

1. Hold up appropriate number of fingers, and then make a fist to indicate total number of words you will pantomine. Get an audible response from your audience before continuing so you know you are communicating.

2. Show which word you will act out first by holding up appropriate number of fingers and making a fist. (*Example:* Two fingers stand for second; fist stands for word. This means you will act out the second word first.) Wait for a response.

3. Indicate the number of syllables in the word by holding up the appropriate number of fingers and chopping your left arm with your right hand. Listen for response.

4. Indicate the syllable you will act out first by holding up the appropriate number of fingers and chopping your left arm with your right hand. Be sure audience is interpreting properly.

5. Proceed to act out words or syllables, whichever give the quickest clues to the answer.

6. Hand pulling ear lobe indicates the answer sounds like what you are acting out. It may rhyme or be similar to what your are pantomiming.

7. Thumb and index finger crooked about one-half inch apart with rest of fingers closed in fist indicates small, unimportant, or connecting words like *a, an, the, and, to.*

8. You are *not* allowed to form letters with your hands, such as forming a *Y* with your legs straight and arms outstretched or forming an *O* with your fingers or arms.

FOCUS   **FOLLOW THE LEADER**

Purpose: To introduce pantomime; to get students warmed up and feeling less self-conscious.

Lead students in pantomime. Tell them to follow your lead, and do as you do. (They feel less shy if you participate, too.) *Example:* I am very warm (look wilted). I am sweating (wipe brow and cheeks). I am walking over to the refrigerator (walk) and opening the door (open door). I am going to stick my head inside to cool off (stick head in; after a few moments start shivering). Continue on, having them imitate your actions in pantomime.

Variations: Say the words to them, and have them react with their own interpretations in pantomime, or read a prepared story that has much action, and have them respond in pantomime.

JOKER   **MIRROR MIME**

Purpose: To develop observation skills; to develop pantomime skills; to have fun.

In this partnership activity the students face each other. One is the leader and one the imitator. As one student does his pantomime, the partner follows his every move as closely as he can. These movements should be spontaneous, rather than planned.

FOCUS   **OBJECT PANTOMIME**

Purpose: To develop imagination and creativity; to develop pantomime skills.

Put an assortment of objects in a pillow case, bag, or box. Have each student reach in (not peeking) and choose one object. Give them ten minutes to prepare a pantomime skit using the object to represent something else in three different ways. They cannot use the object as it would normally be used.

Example: If the object were an old, long-haired woman's wig, the student might use it as a kitten, a floor mop, and a furry muff. The student would need to weave these three objects into a brief skit and pantomime it for the class. The class can guess the three objects represented. You will be amazed at student creativity and humor.

Variation: Students can use their voices instead of being completely silent, and prepare skits using the objects. Insist the object be used three different ways and not as it would normally be utilized.

FOCUS   **FABLE PANTOMIME**

Purpose: To develop pantomime skills; to develop confidence in performing in front of an audience.

Have students choose favorite fables. List on the chalkboard. Decide as a group how many characters they will need for each fable. Have students sign up for the fable of their choice.

Give each group 20 minutes to choose which students are going to play which characters and to plan out their pantomime. Then call on groups to present their fables to the class.

Variation: Students can use their voices instead of being silent, and prepare skits based on fables. (This will require longer preparation time.) If you have students only one class period, they can prepare one day and present the next.

INTRO   **FIRST PANTOMIME**

Purpose: To introduce short and simple patomime; to develop self-confidence in front of a group.

A good first pantomime is acting out everyday activities in pairs. Partnerships help cut down on self-consciousness, and using common activities makes it easy. Students who *pantomime* in front of others FIRST are less frightened to *speak* in front of an audience later. The performance only takes seconds for each pair.

List activities on slips of paper and have them pick them randomly, or have them make up their own activities. The class can guess what they are pantomiming. See *EASY PANTOMIME TOPICS*.

Focus   *EASY PANTOMIME TOPICS*

Instructions to teacher: Run off copies and cut on lines. Put in hat for random drawing for easy first pantomime topics.

playing tennis	cross country skiing
ice skating	building a snowman
getting ready for school	surfing
getting ready for bed	playing basketball
eating breakfast	playing volleyball
playing baseball	playing football
arguing with a friend	going for walk in the rain
playing with dog	shoveling snow
using a computer	doing math homework
playing golf	telephoning a friend
bowling	playing soccer
washing dishes	cleaning up room
riding a skateboard	driving a car
working in the garden	riding a motorcycle
getting ready to go skiing	getting on an airplane

Joker

Purpose: To have fun with pantomime; to get over stage fright.

Instructions: Pretend to be a famous person, an animal, or an object. Act it out in pantomime. The rest of the class will try to guess who or what you are pretending to be. Whoever guesses correctly can do his pantomime next. Your teacher will tell you if you can use your voice for sounds. Choose one of the following or make up your own.

FAMOUS PEOPLE

Michael J. Fox

Madonna

Former President Reagan

George Washington

Johnny Carson

ANIMALS

Bear

Horse

Cat

Duck

Rabbit

OBJECTS

Tree

Table

Motorcycle

Clock

Food blender

FOCUS   **PUPPETS ON A STICK**

Purpose: To create characters; to use characters to present a skit. See MAKE A THEATER for a place to put on the show.

Instructions to students: Cut flat figures of people or animals and paste or glue onto sticks. You can use dowel rods, 12″ rulers, or flat sticks about 12″ long. Use these figures as your characters. You be their voices.

Plan a skit using your characters. Be sure the characters have a problem, several incidents, and a resolution to their dilemma.

Variation: Make bag puppets. Take several paper bags and stuff them appropriately. Tie off a portion for the head and make features on the faces. Leave enough room to get your hand or finger inside the head for some movement during your skit or insert sticks for control.

Variation: Make envelope puppets. Make faces on white or colored envelopes and mount on sticks or put hand inside to control movement.

Variation: Make pipe cleaner characters. Use one pipe cleaner for the heads and two for the bodies. Make them in action poses suitable for your skit. Move them around by hand.

FOCUS   **DISGUISE YOURSELF**

Purpose: To hide behind a mask and be someone or something else; to create a skit and put it on for the class.

Instructions to students: Bring a paper bag large enough to fit comfortably over your head. Decorate the bag as a person or animal. Add yarn hair, eyebrows, eyelashes, or anything else to make it more interesting. Cut out a place for your eyes and mouth so you can see where you are going, and the audience can hear you without your voice being muffled.

Work with a partner to create a skit with your bag character and his. Sit or kneel behind the skirted table (see MAKE A THEATER) with just your bag heads showing. Be sure to move the heads as you speak to make your skit more realistic. Have a dilemma, several incidents, and a conclusion.

Variation: Decorate a paper plate as a character. Attach the plate to your head with a rubber band or string by punching holes near the sides and tieing the bands or string securely. Be sure eye, nose, and mouth holes are cut so you are comfortable and can be heard. Proceed as above.

Variation: Take two pieces of aluminum foil (or one piece of heavy duty foil) and place over your face to form your features. Be sure to close your eyes as you do this. Add hair, hat, or anything else you wish. Hold the masks just above the skirted table or mount them on sticks. Create dialogue and a skit with at least one other person. Proceed as above.

FOCUS   PUTTIN' ON THE SKITS

Purpose: To develop creativity; to have students work cooperatively to develop and participate in a skit for the rest of the class; to develop self-confidence before a group.

Divide class into groups. Have them devise an original skit and put it on for the class. Give them fifteen minutes to plan the skits and five minutes per group to present them.

Variation: Ask them to dramatize the main parts of a story or book. Fairy tales work well.

Variation: Give them three totally unrelated words (nouns), and have students build a skit around them. Be sure to emphasize that the three words must be integral parts of their skit, not incidentally worked in.

Variation: Three groups put on skits on topics of their own choice; other class members tape-record and/or videotape proceedings.

Variation: Have students make up fictional skits based on historical facts. This can follow a literature selection set in an historical period they have studied.

Variation: Have students dramatize a cartoon strip or comic book story. Makeup or costumes add to the fun of this one.

Variation: Have students build a skit around a famous proverb. The best ones usually end with the proverb.

Variation: Give students a "tag line," an ending sentence with which they must conclude their skit. Each group should have a different tag line. It is amazing to see the creative stories they devise! This is fun for the teacher, too. See *TAG LINERS*.

Variation: Have students put on a skit ending with a famous quotation. See *QUOTABLE QUOTES*.

Focus   ***TAG LINERS***

Purpose: To foster creativity; to provide an opportunity to make up an original skit.

Instructions: We will divide into groups of three or four students. After you get into groups, choose one of the following tag lines and make it the ending line of your skit. The tag line must play an important role in the skit and culminate the action. If the tag line can be a surprise or a twist for the audience, so much the better!

1. So that's what he meant by beefsteak!

2. I couldn't have done it better myself!

3. Why, oh why, does it always happen to me?

4. And they call him "Muscles"?

5. Baby, it's cold outside!

6. My Arthur-itis is acting up again!

7. But Bozo—you promised!

8. We always get our man!

9. Run for your life!

Purpose: To foster creativity; to provide an opportunity to make up an original skit.

Instructions to students: We will divide into groups of three or four students. After you get into groups, choose one of the following famous quotations and make it either the ending line of your skit or an important line elsewhere in the skit. If the quotation can carry a punch and have meaning for the audience, rather than seem contrived or trivial, your skit will be more successful.

1. "Why do you laugh? Change but the name, and the story is told of you." (from Horace: *Satires*)

2. "It is easier to stay out than to get out." (from Twain: *Pudd'nhead Wilson's New Calendar*)

3. "Many that are first shall be last; and the last first." (from Mark 10:31)

4. "Something is rotten in the state of Denmark." (from Shakespeare: *Hamlet*)

5. "He could fiddle all the bugs off a sweet-potato-vine." (from Benet: *The Mountain Whippoorwill*)

6. "A fool always finds a greater fool to admire him." (from Boileau: *L'Art Poetique*)

7. "A joke's a very serious thing." (from Churchill: *The Ghost*)

8. "Whatever folly kings commit, the people suffer." (from Horace: *Epistles*)

9. "Ask me no questions, and I'll tell you no fibs." (from Goldsmith: *She Stoops to Conquer*)

10. "Nature speaks in symbols and in signs." (from Whittier: *To Charles Sumner*)

Purpose: To use hands to express thoughts and emotions; to develop imagination; to put on a skit.

Instructions: Choose one of the following and devise a clever skit to present to the class either in pantomime or using dialogue. You can be one of the characters in your skit (if you wish) by talking to your character or characters.

(1) Find expressive ways to move your hands. (They can hug, hit, etc.) Use each hand as one character.

(2) Use tight-fitting gloves (perhaps one white and one black) for your hand characters.

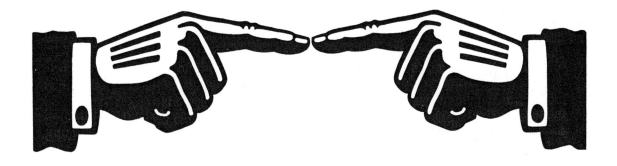

(3) Use two shoes (perhaps not a pair) to represent two characters. Embellish the shoes with facial features or other enhancements. Develop a conversation between them, and present to the class.

(4) Make a fish with your non-writing hand. Put your forefinger over your thumb so the space between your knuckle and thumb forms a moveable mouth. Paint on eyes in the appropriate spots, put lipstick around the mouth to emphasize it, and use your hand as a character. If you want to use both hands as characters, you will need help getting the facial features drawn on.

Purpose: To gain confidence in being in front of others; to learn to "think on your feet" (improvise); to work cooperatively.

Instructions: You are going to act out two skits with a partner. In one you will lead; in one, you will follow. The trick is that the follower is not going to know what the leader is going to do. He must follow the leader and play along in the skit. The teacher will assign a partner just before your act.

1. Decide what character you are.

2. Decide where your scene takes place.

3. Decide who your partner represents.

4. Decide what is going to happen.

5. Jot these items down in the spaces provided below.

6. Hand sheet to the teacher before your improvisation.

When you are the follower, follow along with your partner's dialogue and actions in the most natural way. You hope you will figure out who you are and what is happening partway through the skit!

When you are the leader, try to lead well by giving clues to help your partner follow along. Remember, your partner is completely depending on you for his actions and dialogue.

YOUR CHARACTER_____

SETTING_____

PARTNER'S CHARACTER_____

INCIDENTS _____

_____

_____

_____

_____

PLEASE DO NOT SHARE YOUR PLAN WITH ANYONE IN THE ROOM. IT WILL BE MORE FUN THAT WAY! REMEMBER, THIS IS A TRICKY IMPROVISATION.

FOCUS   EFFECTIVE SOUNDS

Purpose: To learn how to make realistic sound effects; to use sound effects for live and recorded skits, readings, and plays.

Try to get your science department to rig up a simple two-bell (or one buzzer and one bell) system for you. Students can use this for telephone and doorbell sounds. (It often keeps a virtual non-reader productively busy during a play, and you will find it indispensable for adding realism.)

Students usually vie for the chance to be the sound effects person, and it is more difficult than it sounds (no pun intended). The sound effects person needs to be extremely alert to the dialogue and action in the skit or play in order to produce the desired effects at the crucial moment! If he loses his place in the script, the class will cajole him into paying closer attention the next time.

Have wooden blocks available to tromp for people walking. Have glasses to clink, sandpaper to scratch with other objects, a metal dish pan to clang, aluminum foil to crunch for lightning, and various other objects to make different sounds. Students are great at thinking up novel and appropriate sound effects using their voices, bodies (!), and props.

Every time there is a skit, assign specific students to carry out the sound effects. They enjoy it and are excellent at creating just the right sound for the occasion.

JOKER   SILLY SOUNDS

Purpose: To have fun with sound effects.

Have students create a story with absurd sound effects. An expressive reader can read the script with the sound effects persons hidden. Sounds should be made behind a curtain or other blocker with the use of a microphone. The effect is startling and humorous.

The rest of the class is the audience. The audience should NOT see the rehearsals for this project so the surprise element of the humor is maintained. This activity is a big hit with a creative class.

Variation: Use *SILLY SOUNDS STORY*.

Purpose: To have fun with sound effects.

Instructions: Prepare to read orally the following story to the class. Have behind-the-scenes partners making the silly sound effects. Be sure to rehearse enough to make a smooth and humorous presentation. If you can improve the story or sound effects, use your creativity and ingenuity to do so.

If you are not involved in this silly sounds story, your group will make up your own story (or find a suitable one) and arrange for sound effects needed to make it interesting or humorous.

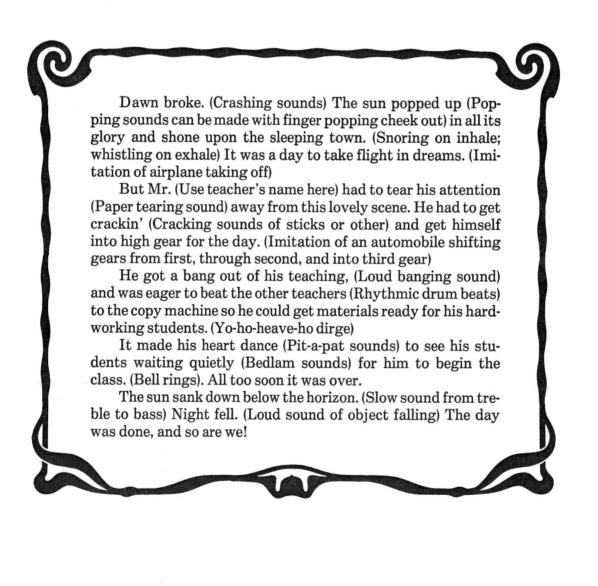

Dawn broke. (Crashing sounds) The sun popped up (Popping sounds can be made with finger popping cheek out) in all its glory and shone upon the sleeping town. (Snoring on inhale; whistling on exhale) It was a day to take flight in dreams. (Imitation of airplane taking off)

But Mr. (Use teacher's name here) had to tear his attention (Paper tearing sound) away from this lovely scene. He had to get crackin' (Cracking sounds of sticks or other) and get himself into high gear for the day. (Imitation of an automobile shifting gears from first, through second, and into third gear)

He got a bang out of his teaching, (Loud banging sound) and was eager to beat the other teachers (Rhythmic drum beats) to the copy machine so he could get materials ready for his hard-working students. (Yo-ho-heave-ho dirge)

It made his heart dance (Pit-a-pat sounds) to see his students waiting quietly (Bedlam sounds) for him to begin the class. (Bell rings). All too soon it was over.

The sun sank down below the horizon. (Slow sound from treble to bass) Night fell. (Loud sound of object falling) The day was done, and so are we!

HOW-TO SPEECH

Purpose: To learn to speak more effectively in front of a group; to explain how to do something in a logical sequence.

Instructions: A how-to speech is sometimes called a demonstration speech. Demonstrate how to do something by bringing in an object or making a visual aid, and providing an explanation.

You can choose one of the following topics or show how to do something else about which you are more knowledgeable. Try to go into enough depth with your topic that others will learn something new, rather than repeat what your classmates already know.

1. Bring in a golf club and demonstrate, physically and in the speech, how to putt, drive, and chip.

2. Bring in crochet needles and thread, and show, physically and in the speech, how to do several stitches. Show several finished projects.

3. Make a drawing of a football field on poster board or chalkboard. Explain several plays that football players use by words and reference to the diagram.

4. Bring in art materials and show how to draw while explaining the technique.

5. Bring in a musical instrument, explain how notes are obtained on it, and demonstrate how to play it.

6. Bring in a tennis racket and demonstrate the proper grip for forehand and backhand. Show the correct way to serve and volley, and explain the basics of scoring.

7. Sketch an ice hockey rink on poster board or the chalkboard. Explain how the game is played, what equipment is needed, and the scoring.

8. Give a talk about horses, demonstrating grooming materials and how to use them, explaining the trappings needed for riding, and other specifics on horse care.

IMPROMPTU SPEECH

Purpose: To learn to speak in front of a group with virtually no preparation; to learn to "think on your feet," not necessarily give a polished speech.

Instructions: Think of two topics which anyone can easily speak about for a brief time, and write them on separate scraps of paper. The subjects should not be embarrassing. We will collect them and put them in a container. Be careful what you suggest. You may have to speak on your own topic!

We are going to put the topics in a hat or box. You will draw out a topic and give a one-minute talk to the class with only a moment to collect your thoughts. (You will have to stand in front of the class for the entire minute whether or not you are speaking!)

If you pick a topic that is impossible for you to speak on, you may say, "Pass!" and return it to the box. If you choose to pass, you will have no further choice. The teacher will choose one of the following topics for you:

My Pet (or The Pet I'd Like)
Brothers (or Sisters)
My Favorite Class (or Least Favorite Class)
My Most Embarrassing Moment (or Most Frightening)
My Favorite Movie (or Television Show)
Parents
My Favorite Aunt (or Uncle, Cousin)
My Best Friend
My Favorite Teacher

Focus

ACCEPTING AN AWARD

Name _____ **Date** _____

Purpose: To learn how to graciously accept an award or honor.

Instructions: Prepare a brief (less than a minute) speech accepting an honor or award. Choose one of the listed topics, and pretend you have just been presented with the award. You may make up your own award.

Remember, acknowledge the importance of the award and your appreciation, but be humble. The acceptance should be short. Use the lines below to plan your acceptance speech, but speak without notes in front of the class.

- Trophy for winning a tennis match
- One hundred dollar bond for winning an essay contest
- Certificate for good citizenship
- Certificate for perfect attendance
- Award for selling the most magazines in school contest
- Dictionary for winning spelling bee
- Medal for outstanding track performance

_____

_____

_____

_____

_____

_____

_____

_____

_____

_____

_____

_____

_____

Focus   *ORAL REPORT*

Name _____   **Date** _____

Purpose: To give an informational talk; to tell in your own words information you have looked up in reference material.

Instructions: Prepare a three-minute talk that will provide information for your class-mates. Use an encyclopedia, book, or other material to locate your facts.

You will be given one class period to locate material, take notes, and organize your facts. We will spend the class period in the library so you have many sources available. You may choose any topic you feel would interest others, and can use your notes as you speak. Your notes *must* be in your own words. Use this sheet and the back of this sheet for your notes.

_____

_____

_____

_____

_____

_____

_____

_____

_____

_____

_____

_____

_____

_____

_____

_____

Focus   ***ENCYCLOPEDIA TALK***

Name _____ Date _____

Purpose: To learn to comprehend factual material; to put the main ideas into your own words; to give a three-minute informational speech.

Instructions: Encyclopedias will be passed out at random. You are to take the encyclopedia, quickly find an interesting topic, and jot down notes on the material. You may NOT trade encyclopedias with anyone else. Use this sheet to gather notes *in your own words.*

_____

_____

_____

_____

_____

_____

_____

_____

_____

_____

_____

_____

                _____

                _____

                _____

                _____

                _____

                _____

Focus ***NEWSPAPER REPORT****

Name _____ **Date** _____

Purpose: To learn to comprehend factual material; to put the main ideas into your own words; to give a three-minute informational speech.

Instructions: Newspapers or parts of newspapers will be passed out at random. You are to take the newspaper, quickly find an interesting topic, and jot down notes on the material. You may NOT trade newspapers with anyone else. Use this sheet to gather notes *in your own words.*

Focus   ***RECITATION***

Purpose: To memorize a notable piece of poetry or prose; to recite it to an audience.

Instructions: Pick one of the following famous writings. Memorize it and rehearse it to recite to the class. If you prefer another writing, get it approved by your teacher.

"We, the people of the United States, in order to form a more perfect union, establish justice, insure domestic tranquillity, provide for the common defence, promote the general welfare, and secure the blessings of liberty to ourselves and our posterity, do ordain and establish this Constitution for the United States of America." (*Preamble to the Constitution of the United States*)

". . . from these honored dead we take increased devotion to that cause for which they gave the last full measure of devotion; that we here highly resolve that these dead shall not have died in vain; that this nation, under God, shall have a new birth of freedom, and that government of the people, by the people, for the people, shall not perish from the earth." (*From Lincoln's "Gettysburg Address"*)

"Give me your tired, your poor,
Your huddled masses yearning to breathe free,
The wretched refuse of your teeming shore.
Send these, the homeless, tempest-tost to me,
I lift my lamp beside the golden door!" (*From Emma Lazarus's poem on the tablet in main entrance to the pedestal of the Statue of Liberty*)

"To every thing there is a season, and a time to every purpose under the heaven:
A time to be born, and a time to die; a time to plant and a time to pluck up that which is planted;
A time to kill, and a time to heal; a time to break down, and a time to build up;
A time to weep, and a time to laugh; a time to mourn, and a time to dance;
A time to cast away stones, and a time to gather stones together; a time to embrace, and a time to refrain from embracing;
A time to get, and a time to lose; a time to keep, and a time to cast away;
A time to rend, and a time to sew; a time to keep silence, and a time to speak;
A time to love, and a time to hate; a time of war, and a time of peace."

(*Ecclesiastes 3:1–9*)

Focus   ***TRUST ME—I'M RIGHT***

Name _____   **Date** _____

Purpose: To give a persuasive speech; to try to change someone's mind on an issue.

Instructions: Choose any opinion you feel strongly about. Prepare a defense of that opinion, stating at least three strong reasons why you are right. Elaborate on each point, and try to persuade others to your opinion. The speech should last between two and three minutes. Make notes below.

Opening statement _____

_____

First reason _____

_____

_____

_____

Second reason _____

_____

_____

_____

Third reason _____

_____

_____

_____

Closing statement _____

_____

_____

Variation: Give a speech to advertise a product or service. Try to convince others to buy the product or service. These speeches will be briefer, but can be humorous and exciting.

FOCUS   MAKE A THEATER

Purpose: To encourage creativity; to provide a place to showcase original skits and shows.

Make the theater from a large cardboard box. Have a cutout area in the front to display the action of puppets or other characters. Insert a dowel rod sideways to hang a split curtain to pull when opening and closing scenes, or mount a window shade. These should be controlled from the upstage (back) side of the box.

The box should sit securely on a planning table which is large enough for students to sit behind comfortably. The table can be covered with roll paper on three sides (front and two sides) from tabletop to floor to conceal the students. Students can name the theater and print its name near the top on the front.

If you string a wire across from side to side, you can attach invisible thread to the ankles and arms of your puppets to help make their actions more lively. The wire should not show, but be above the "stage" area.

This makeshift theater provides a place for puppets, mask characters, glove characters, pipe cleaner people, etc. to act out skits. The students (usually two) behind the table control the action.

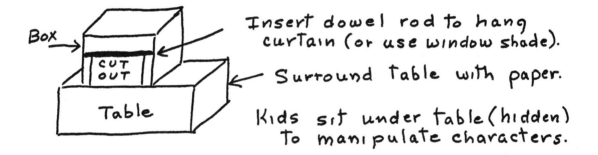

JOKER   COSTUMES

Purpose: To have fun performing oral skits, improvisations, and "dress up."

Collect clothing and props of all sorts for use in your class. Minimals include an assortment of hats (witch's hat, baseball cap, golf hat, and others), cane, wigs, dishes, high heels, telephones, old dresses, tray, long dowel rod (this is versatile), toy gun, apron, shawl, towel, jackets or coats, and fake mustache and beard. You can begin the collection, and students will contribute items during the year until you have a variety. Just adding a hat makes a student feel more like the character he is portraying and definitely adds to the flavor and fun of student presentations.

Focus   ***STAGE DIRECTIONS***

Name _____   Date _____

Purpose: To learn basic stage directions; to learn to follow oral directions.

A stage is divided into nine basic areas for ease in giving instructions to actors for stage positions. All areas are from the point of view of the performer facing the audience. That is, left refers to the performer's left as he stands facing the house. Downstage is the area closest to the audience; upstage is the area to the back of the stage farthest away from the audience. Abbreviations commonly used are:

L = Left; R = Right; C = Center; U = Upstage; D = Downstage

Instructions: Study the designated stage areas. Write out a series of five stage directions to give to another student orally. Be prepared to follow stage directions yourself.

UR	UC	UL
CR	C	CL
DR	DC	DL

On the lines below write two series of directions.

Example:

Go to DR. Kneel.   _____   _____

Cross to UL.   _____   _____

Go to C. Twirl.   _____   _____

Go to DL.   _____   _____

Cross to UR. Bow.   _____   _____

© 1990 by The Center for Applied Research in Education

FOCUS   TEACHER FOR A DAY

Purpose: To give students experience in presenting factual information to a group; to build self-image; to involve students directly in the teaching-learning process.

This project involves minimal teacher intervention and maximal student involvement. You will arrange the sequence of the student presentations, score the tests, if any, and serve as a resource to the various groups. Other than this, you will try to allow students autonomy and freedom. (This is more difficult than it sounds, as it is hard to keep from interfering when you may feel you know a better way. It is important to the success of this project, however, that it be completely student taught.) On the days of presentations, you should sit in a student chair and participate, if at all, as a student. See *TEACHER FOR A DAY*.

The following outline shows typical student time allotment for their five days of in-class planning. It is helpful to place each day's goals on the chalkboard at the beginning of that day's planning session.

Goals: *1st Session* (In Groups)

    Divide into groups.
    Elect chairman and secretary.
    Decide on lesson to be taught.
    Check with teacher after decision on lesson.
    Discuss methods you will use.

Goals: *2nd Session* (In Groups)

    Continue methods discussion.
    Make decisions on who will use which methods.
    Make decisions on which part of lesson each will teach.
    Begin lesson plans, if there is time.

Goals: *3rd Session* (Individual)

    Work on lesson plans.
    Rough out test questions on your section.

Goals: *4th Session* (Individual)

    Prepare materials needed (written handouts, etc.).
    Make any special arrangements (speakers, etc.).

Goals: *5th Session* (In Groups; Final Planning Session)

    Prepare test for class over lesson material.
    Submit test to teacher for safe-keeping.

Purpose: Would you like to trade places with your teacher and teach the class the way YOU think it should be done? Here's your chance!

Instructions:

1. Get into groups; elect a chairman and secretary. The chairman keeps the group orderly and moving toward your goals. The secretary takes notes on each plan session.

2. Select a lesson from the textbook to present to the class. Be sure it is long enough so that each group member can participate actively in the presentation. Your group presentation should last approximately one class period. As soon as you have chosen the lesson, inform the teacher. (First come, first served!)

3. Decide what methods will be best for the presentation. Vary your approach to keep the interest of the class. Methods to consider: guest, skit, interview, game, lecture, discussion, display, work or practice sheets, tape recorder, computer, VCR, movie, slides, records, overhead projector transparencies, opaque projection, bulletin board. Do not feel limited by these.

4. Each person in your group must use a different method of presentation. Decide who will use what method.

5. Each person must present a written lesson plan to the teacher before presentation. You will be given five class periods to prepare. IF YOU NEED MORE TIME, YOU WILL HAVE TO PREPARE OUTSIDE OF CLASS.

6. Prepare and practice your lesson until your timing is accurate, and the lesson flows smoothly.

7. As a group, prepare a test for the class on the material. This can be a standard test or other evaluative measure. Work for an 80 percent mastery level. Students not getting 80 percent or above will have to be given individual help by your group members until they have mastered the lesson. (Do not include time to give the test or extra help for mastery in your lesson presentation time.)

8. You must invite the teacher to at least TWO planning sessions. The teacher will not be involved in your presentations, but feel free to use the teacher as a resource person (to settle disputes, answer technical questions, or to give advice as requested).

Focus   *MA BELL*

Purpose: To show proper telephone usage; to show divergent use dependent upon purposes.

Instructions: Choose a partner and use the unconnected real telephones in the room to engage in mock telephone calls (from dialing through dialogue to hanging up). Both parties should demonstrate proper use, courtesy, and promptness. Choose one of the situations below, and make it sound realistic.

1. You are calling your aunt to thank her for the birthday present of a new sweater.

2. You are calling your friend to find out what the homework assignment is for history class.

3. You are calling your history teacher to find out what the homework assignment is!

4. You are calling a company to complain about the broken toy you received.

5. You are calling the fire department to report a fire.

6. You are calling a friend to chat.

7. You are calling your mother to ask if you can go home after school with your friend.

8. You are calling your father to tell him you broke your leg in gym class.

9. You are calling your grandmother to tell her you just received an *A* on your science test.

10. You are calling a store to find out about computer disks (sizes, prices, discounts for quantity, etc.).

11. You are calling a friend to see if he would like to attend a basketball game with you.

12. You are calling a person to apologize for an incident that happened in school yesterday.

13. You are calling to tell someone they have just won a spot on the cheerleading squad.

Purpose: To encourage deeper thinking about the viewpoint of authors; to encourage curiosity about authors; to learn proper telephone usage; to work cooperatively with others.

Instructions: Choose one of the following three scenarios. Use the rest of the page to jot down possible questions or answers.

1. Call an author of your choice on a mock telephone. Ask questions about the motivation and inspiration for his writing, his personal life, or his thinking about the characters or subject of his writing.

Arrange for a partner to play the role of the author. Both you and your partner need to prepare yourselves in order to carry on a realistic conversation.

2. Call a character in a story and ask relevant questions. You will need another student to prepare to be the part of the other character.

3. Be a character in a story and call a character in ANOTHER story. Again, a partner must prepare to be the other character.

Focus   ***RADIO OR TV BROADCAST***

Purpose: To present a cooperative class project; to work on expression in voice; to build confidence in speaking.

Instructions: Choose a portion of the total project, and work individually or with others to perfect your part. The goal is a tape-recorded, simulated radio broadcast or a video-taped, simulated television broadcast.

Mark your first and second choices of the following parts by putting a *1* by your first and a *2* by your second choice. Your papers will be collected and assignments made to coincide as closely to your wishes as possible, while still maintaining typical variety for a day's broadcast possibilities.

__ Drama

__ Public service announcement

__ Soap opera

__ Commercials (advertisements)

__ Talk show monologue

__ News

__ Man-on-the-street interview

__ Game show

__ Disk jockey segment (musical interludes involving student talent, not recordings)

__ Sports announcing (contest in progress)

__ On-the-spot reporting (disaster or event in progress)

__ Time-of-day and station-identification patter

__ Sports (wrap-up of day's action and scores)

__ Radio or TV spots (brief announcements)

__ Weather

__ Talk show interview (how about an author?)

Presentations for television with use of a video camera and playback on videotape are more difficult than cassette-recorded radio broadcasts. The visual aspect means more line memorization, planning for video impact, and instruction on equipment.

Focus   *TELEVISION ANALYSIS*

Name _____ Date _____

Purpose: To determine setting, plot, characters, and theme; to analyze a televised or videotaped drama as you would a novel that you read; to present an oral report.

Instructions: Watch a television show or videotape of at least a half hour in length. Fill out the pertinent information below and deliver it orally to the class.

NAME OF SHOW _____

SETTING _____

NAME AND DESCRIBE EACH CHARACTER. DO NOT USE ACTORS' NAMES.

_____

_____

_____

_____

MAJOR PLOT (INCLUDE MAIN PROBLEM, INCIDENTS, AND SOLUTION)

_____

_____

_____

_____

_____

_____

THEME _____

CRITIQUE (WHY YOU LIKED/ DID NOT LIKE SHOW)

_____

_____

Purpose: To show varying moods and meanings by voice; to experiment with voice expression.

Instructions: Words or phrases change meanings by the way we say them. Practice the following expressions, trying to give the desired meaning shown in parentheses. Use variation in speed, tone, style, facial expression, and voice inflection.

When everyone has had a chance to practice, we'll call on you to recite one or two expressions. The rest of the class will guess which one you are attempting to get across.

1. Yes! (emphatic)
    Yes? (questioning)
    Yeessss? (sarcastic)
    Y-y-yes. (frightened)
    Yes. (shy; tentative)

2. Oh, yeah. (understanding)
    Oh, yeah. (defiant)
    Oh, yeah! (happy)
    Oh, yeah. (sarcastic)

3. *Now* is the time.
    Now *is* the time.
    Now is *the* time.
    Now is the *time.*

4. No! (emphatic)
    No? (questioning)
    No-o-o. (unbelieving)
    N-n-no. (stuttering)
    No-oo. (sarcastic)

5. *This* is the end.
    This *is* the end.
    This is *the* end.
    This is the *end.*

6. *What* do you mean?
    What *do* you mean?
    What do *you* mean?
    What do you *mean?*

7. *You* look great. (as opposed to someone else)
    You *look* great. (implying you don't feel great)
    You look *great.* (sincerely)

Section V

ANSWER KEY

SECTION I (Writing and Composition)

BE, CLEAR DEAR

Suggested improvements (others possible):

1. When I was ten, my parents got divorced.
2. The cat he bought from the man turned out to be a short-haired tabby.
3. The lady I talked to by the telephone pole reminded me of you.
4. Since it was a sunny day, we ended up sitting under an umbrella near the fountain.
5. Long before, Charlie had left everything to the brother he loved dearly.
6. The burly boy in a black hat bumped into the elephant.
7. The pig pen of the man that used to be our friend was painted yesterday.
8. I walked along the dock swinging my duffel bag as the boat sailed into port.
9. Just as the quiet lady opened the door, the band used six trumpets to play the school fight song.
10. When the radiator boiled over, the driver stopped his truck and asked for water.

WHICH CAME FIRST—THE CHICKEN OR THE EGG?

listened to loud rock music—lost hearing
didn't study—got poor grade
ate too much—got stomachache
chicken—egg
studied hard—passed test
set ladder on ice—fell
went on diet—lost 3 pounds
egg—chicken
was late to class—had to report to office
wrote a letter to friend—received a letter
forgot to feed cat—cat ran away
gave up hard candy—had no cavities

LETTER LITERACY

Riddle answers:

1. Yes, but it'll be easier to read if you use paper!
2. *POST OFFICE*

SCRAMBLED EGGS (unscrambled)

Note: The order in which the student lists the details (A, B, C, etc.) is not important as long as the details are under the right topic.

I.   Ways to Prepare
     A. Poached
     B. Scrambled
     C. Boiled
     D. Fried
II. Colors
     A. Brown
     B. White
III. Advantages
     A. Inexpensive
     B. Low calories
     C. High protein
IV. Disadvantages
     A. Allergenic
     B. High cholesterol

NAME THAT POEM

Riddle Answer: Your name

PROOF IS IN THE PUDDING

1. John and Mary are brother and *sister.*
2. They have three pet *dogs* which they *love dearly.*
3. John calls one dog Spot because he has several *spots* on his back.
4. Another he calls *Blackie* because of his *dark* color.
5. The *big* dog is Mary's favorite.
6. One day the *kids* and all the *dogs* went on a *hike* to the woods.
7. They saw the squirrels *run,* the rabbits *hop,* and the *birds* fly.
8. When they got *home,* they decided to *make* some pudding.
9. John *wanted* to make chocolate, but Mary preferred *custard.*
10. Finally, they agreed to *make* a *batch* of *butterscotch.*

SECTION II (Reading and Literature)

SAME OR DIFFERENT

(1) S (2) S (3) D (4) S (5) D (6) D (7) D (8) D (9) S (10) D (11) D (12) S

WHAT IS OUT OF PLACE?

(1) nail (2) November (3) woman (4) fingers (5) finger (6) elephant (7) glass (8) book (9) movie (10) cousin (11) celery (12) Jane

FOLLOWING DIRECTIONS (Easy Paper/Pencil Version)

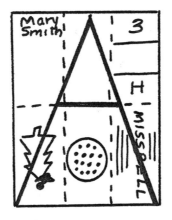

FOLLOWING DIRECTIONS (Difficult Paper/Pencil Version)

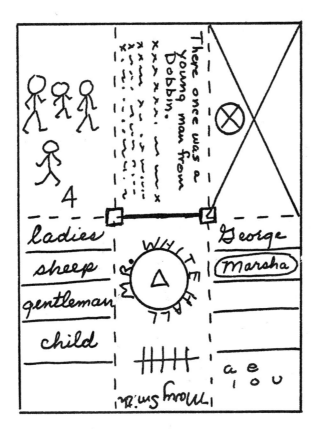

YOUNG, OLD, OR IN-BETWEEN?

1, 2, 3, 5, 8, 9, 10 (Yes); 4, 6, 7 (No)

CATS

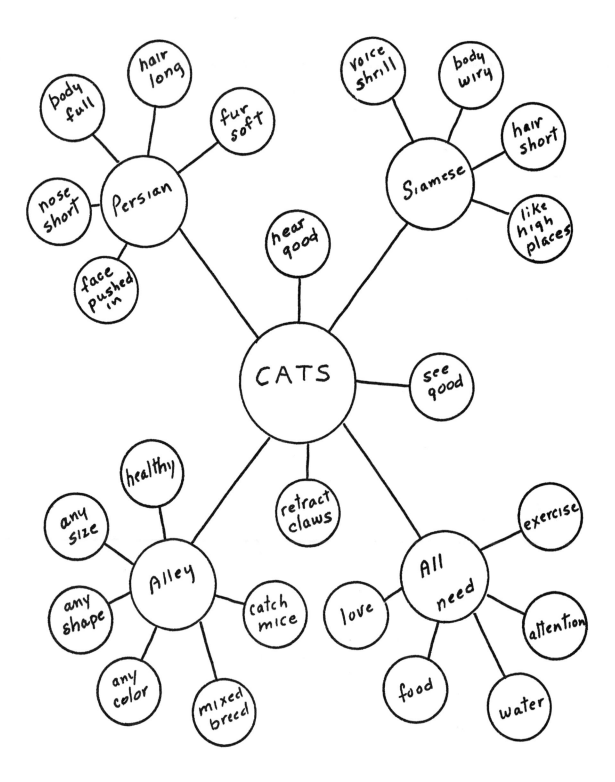

INCOMPLETE RHYMES

fat, floor, ring, lake, pail, right, pan, hill, look, bang, gold, cake, night, short, time

ADD-A-LETTER RHYME

1. fraction, reaction, faction, satisfaction, traction
2. nation, ration, creation, elation, inflation, rotation
3. motion, commotion, potion, lotion, notion, devotion
4. launch, paunch, haunch, staunch
5. biology, psychology, technology, ecology, etymology
6. dealer, sealer, healer, stealer
7. dancer, prancer, cancer, lancer
8. section, election, convection, confection, direction
9. wobble, cobble, gobble, hobble, bobble
10. crawl, drawl, trawl, brawl, scrawl

SECTION III (Words and Sentences)

ABOMINABLE ABBREVIATIONS and *ABBREVIATION VARIATION*

1. Wyoming (WY) = Why
    Colonel (Col.) = call
    telephone (tel.) = tell
    peninsula (pen.) = pen
    person (pers.) = purse
    Saturday (Sat.) = sat

2. catalog (cat.) = cat
    history (hist.) = hissed
    Maine (ME) = me
    Friday (Fri) = fry
    inch (in.) = in
    Sunday (Sun.) = sun

3. January (Jan.) = Jan
    Madam (Mad.) = mad
    Maximum (Max.) = Max
    gazetteer (gaz.) = gas
    Reverend (Rev.) = rev

4. Number (no.) = no
    Wednesday (Wed.) = wed
    Dozen (Doz.) = does
    library (lib.) = lib
    science (sci.) = sigh
    pseudonym (pseud.) = sued

5. record (rec.) = wreck
    numbers (nos.) = nose

number (num.) = numb
Fahrenheit (Fahr.) = fair or far

6. society (soc.) = sock
    capital (cap.) = cap
    Arizona (AZ) = as
    singular (sing.) = sing

7. Massachusetts (MA) = Ma
    Pennsylvania (PA) = Pa
    Alabama (AL) = Al
    Illinois (IL) = ill

8. Idaho (ID) = I'd
    Hawaii (HI) = Hi
    answer (ans.) = aunts
    Wyoming (WY) = why
    Ohio (OH) = oh
    Wisconsin (WI) = why
    synonym (syn.) = sin

STATE IT

Correct postal abbreviations for the fifty states of the United States of America:

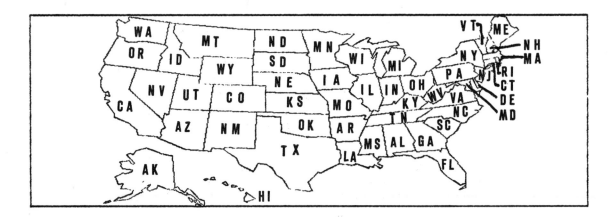

GUESS THE AFFIX

un = not; pre = before; in = not; sub = under; mis = wrongly; hood = state of; ism = system of; ness = state of; less = without; ant = that does

COMMON ROOTS AND AFFIXES

Eighty-four of the words from these prefix, root, and suffix combinations are as follows:

childhood	childish	deprogram	detract
childless	deform	description	detraction

distract	joyous	pretreat	subscript
distraction	kinder	preview	subscription
disuse	kindly	programmable	subtract
enjoy	kindness	programmer	subtraction
enjoyable	misuse	protract	tractable
entreat	mistreat	protraction	traction
former	movable	reform	treatable
formless	movement	reformer	treatment
friendly	mover	reheat	unfriendly
friendless	overheat	remove	unkind
heatable	overjoy	reprogram	unkindly
heater	overuse	retract	unkindness
heatless	overview	retractable	unusable
informant	perform	retraction	usable
informer	performance	retreat	useful
inscription	performer	reusable	useless
intractable	peruse	reuse	user
joyful	preheat	review	viewable
joyless	prescription	reviewer	viewer

ANAGRAM ANOMALY

vile = evil; laid = dial; reed = deer; teacher = cheater; saw = was; cheat = teach; oh = ho; dear = read; said = dias or aids; now = won.
(Sometimes your dyslexic kids do especially well on this.)

CAN A CAT BECOME A DOG?

(1) cat (2) live (3) house (4) bay; may (5) cot; cog (6) rail (7) pep; pea (8) boat; beat (9) have; cave; cove (10) foil; fail

GETTING ACQUAINTED WITH ANTONYMS

*d*own-up	*m*other-father
*t*each-*l*earn	*h*eat-cold
tiny-hug*e*	bright-*d*ark
whit*e*-*b*lack	*w*omen-me*n*
*a*part-together	*d*anger-safety
*f*all-rise	man*y*-few
open-*c*lose	*h*ate-love
*b*ought-*s*old	*t*all-short
scow*l*-smile	lad*y*-gentleman
*t*ear-men*d*	*s*our-sweet

GETTING BRANDED

Band Aid adhesive, Apple computer, Bic pen, Bold detergent, Coke bottle, Ford car, Gem paper clips, General Electric refrigerator, Harley-Davidson motorcycle, Ivory soap, Joy dishwashing liquid, Kodak camera, Levi jeans, Prell shampoo, Prentice Hall book, Royal typewriter, Scott tissue, Trapper Keeper note-book, Xerox copier, Schwinn bicycle

CAN YOU DE-CODE DE CODE?

Cryptic proverbs:

He who laughs last laughs best.
You may delay, but time will not.
Spare the rod and spoil the child.

Coded message:

You may leave the room, get a drink, and go to the rest room.
Substitutions: Y=a; O=c; U=o; M=z; E=x; R=p; N=l

MIND-BOGGLERS

Poem with vowels left out:

    I never saw a purple cow;
    I never hope to see one;
    But I can tell you anyhow,
    I'd rather see than be one.

One solution to pyramid puzzle:

a, at, mat, team, meats, stream, masters

USING THE SCHWA

cafeteria; custody, narrative, author

BASIC SENTENCE PATTERNS

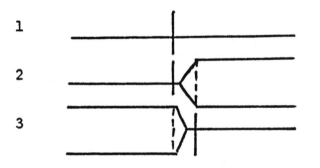

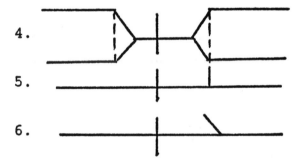

ACTION MAN CAN

Fifteen action verbs should be circled: run, moo, think, growl, bark, look, break, shout, see, dance, compute, jump, hiss, play, dream

PRO-CROSS

Across:		Down:	
	2. it		1. you
	5. they		2. it
	7. him		3. them
	8. us		4. you
	10. me		6. you
	11. I		7. he
	12. we		9. she
	13. her		

DOUBLE TROUBLE

Some possibilities:

T=letter, better, setter; S=lesson, session, floss; L=telling, selling, mill; E=seed, greed, free; A=bazaar; W=powwow; K=bookkeeper, jackknife; I=skiing; U=vacuum; Z=jazz, buzzard, blizzard

Word with 26 letters is *alphabet*!

Word with *q* not followed by *u* is *qiviut*, meaning the wool of the musk ox's undercoat.

ALPHABET SOUP

T; U and I; Q; C; O; B; P; I-C; I-V; U; Y; I; G; J; R; L; M; I-Q; K, D, M, B, K-T; C-D

WORDS WITHIN WORDS

(1) giant (2) pigmy; also spelled pygmy, but pygmy is incorrect because it does not have *pig* in it (3) bullet (4) porcupine (5) trumpet (6) horseradish (7) oxygen (8) catapult (9) catalog (10) coward (11) puppet (12) goatee (13) catalpa (14) dogwood (15) bugle (16) kite

RIDDLE FUN

(1) lilac (2) George (3) tulips (4) daffodil (5) loon (6) Cardinal (7) crane (8) palm (9) pear (10) apple (11) crab (12) orange (13) locust (14) doughnut (15) beechnut (16) walnut (17) peanut (18) Hazelnut (19) cashew (20) Brazil

SECTION IV (Speaking, Listening, and Oral Presentation)

COMMUNICATION SCRAMBLE

(1) telephone (2) tree blaze (3) letter (4) sign language (5) radio (6) Morse code (7) hieroglyphics (8) book (9) television (10) videotape (11) smoke signal (12) drum beat (13) newspaper (14) voice (15) telegraph (16) magazine (17) telegram (18) body language (19) gesture (20) movie